ION

KA'S

ND POLAR BEARS

ARS

IERWONIT

M WALKER

ASKA
THWEST
OOKS®

For the bears and all those people who do good work on their behalf.

Acknowledgments—I thank the many bear biologists who have shared their knowledge with me over the years. For this revised and updated edition of *Alaska's Bears*, I'm especially grateful to Sean Farley, Anthony Pagano, and Tom Smith. I also remain thankful to the researchers and managers who helped me while I worked on the original book: Steve Amstrup, Larry Aumiller, Gerald Garner, John Hechtel, Sterling Miller, Scott Schliebe, and Chuck Schwartz. I also appreciate the help that cultural anthropologist Richard Nelson provided during my initial work. I thank Doug Pfeiffer for seeing the merits of doing an updated version of this book, Kathy Howard for her work on its production, and Vicki Knapton for its design. Finally, I honor the bears, who continue to be an inspiration and blessing in my life.

Text © 1998, 2016 by Bill Sherwonit
Photographs © 1998, 2016 by Tom Walker

Library of Congress Cataloging-in-Publication Data
Names: Sherwonit, Bill, 1950-
Title: Alaska's bears : grizzlies, black bears, and polar bears / text by Bill Sherwonit ; photographs by Tom Walker.
Description: Portland, OR : Alaska Northwest Books, [2016] | Originally published: 1998. | Includes bibliographical references and index.
Identifiers: LCCN 2015050637 | ISBN 9781943328581 (pbk.) | ISBN 9781943328598 (hardbound) | ISBN 9781943328567 (e-book)
Subjects: LCSH: Grizzly bear—Alaska. | Black bear—Alaska. | Polar bear—Alaska.
Classification: LCC QL737.C27 S5 2016 | DDC 599.78409798—dc23 LC record available at http://lccn.loc.gov/2015050637

Cover: Brown bear on spring sedge flats, Alaska Peninsula.
Back cover: Alaska is home to all three North American bears: black, grizzly, and polar.
Pages 1: Female brown bear and first year cub in late summer; 2: Kenai Peninsula black bear scenting the air; 3: Polar bears sparring in early winter snow; 6: Black bear in Southcentral Alaska; 12–13: Polar bear and cub of the year in early winter; 36–37: Two yearling brown bears warily watch an approaching bear; 64–65: Black bear struts in territorial display; 84: Brown bear catching red salmon on Brooks Falls, Katmai; 88: Brown bear with a red salmon caught in Mikfik Creek, near McNeil River.

Updated design: Vicki Knapton
Maps: Gray Mouse Graphics; US Fish and Wildlife Service
Illustrations (pages 62-63) © by Richard Carstensen

Alaska Northwest Books®
An imprint of

GRAPHIC ARTS
BOOKS®

P.O. Box 56118
Portland, OR 97238-6118
(503) 254-5591
www.graphicartsbooks.com

CONTENTS

BEAR COUNTRY

The sight of the bear stirred me like nothing else the country could contain. What mattered was not so much the bear himself as what the bear implied. He was the predominant thing in that country, and for him to be in it at all meant that there had to be more country like it in every direction and more of the same kind of country all around that. He implied a world.

—John McPhee, *Coming into the Country* (1976)

I first saw a wild bear in 1974, during my first month in Alaska. A chocolate-colored grizzly, it stood several hundred yards away, busily digging into the tundra for roots or perhaps ground squirrels. Like John McPhee, I saw the grizzly while exploring the Brooks Range wilderness, though I'd come not as a writer but as a 24-year-old geologist recently out of graduate school. And like McPhee, I was deeply stirred by the sight of this bear. But what moved me was the grizzly itself, rather than anything it implied about wildness or vast, undeveloped landscapes. A fuller appreciation of that connection would come later.

Even now I can recall the mix of awe, delight, and fear that I felt, the desire to know more about grizzlies. About bears. Still, I couldn't have realized the extent to which bears—both as physical beings and as metaphors—would become a fascination of mine, a passion.

This black bear has left the forest to search the tundra for blueberries.

I eventually left Alaska for California, but returned in 1982, now a writer. Two things, above all others, drew me back: wild landscapes and wildlife. I suppose you could say I wanted to be closer to the bear's world and all that implies.

Like many people who live here, I sometimes call Alaska "bear country"—for good reason. Alaska is the only one of our nation's 50 states to be inhabited by all three of North America's ursine species: the black bear, polar bear, and brown bear (also known as the grizzly). Alaska's population of all three bears remains healthy midway into the second decade of the 21st century, thanks largely to Alaska's abundance of wild, remote, and undeveloped regions, though the future of the polar bear is clouded by climate change (more on that below).

There are few places you can go in Alaska and not share the landscape with bears. Even Anchorage, with more than 300,000 people, is visited seasonally by black and brown bears that inhabit the tundra and forests along its edges. I've discovered that the presence of bears, even if unseen, changes my relationship with a place: it makes me more attentive, more aware of my surroundings.

Alaska offers some of the world's best bear viewing. Managed programs at places like McNeil River, Brooks River, and Admiralty Island and an abundance of commercial bear-viewing operations elsewhere give even backcountry neophytes a chance to safely watch wild bears in their natural environments.

As one who loves both bears and literature, I've lined my bookshelves with dozens of bear books. But until the original publication of *Alaska's Bears*, there hadn't been a book specifically about Alaska's bears that fits the category of field guide, a book that slips easily into a jacket pocket or day pack—and one that also provides entertaining armchair reading for when you're not in bear country. Even now, nearly two decades later, the book remains unique. Here, in one compact edition, is a book that can help you understand Alaska's bears and their natural histories. Chapters on each of the three species cover their physical appearance, behaviors, yearly cycles, ecological niches, and relationships with humans. One chapter looks at Alaska's prime bear-viewing sites, with full details for those who would like to learn more and possibly visit. You'll also find tips for traveling safely through bear country. And this new, updated guidebook presents the most current understandings of bears and our species' relationship with them. Complementing the text are the photographs of longtime Alaskan Tom Walker, a premier wildlife photographer who has spent hundreds of hours in the company of bears.

For nearly three-and-a-half decades now, I've shared the Alaskan landscape with bears in places that range from lush coastal rain forests to high alpine valleys to Arctic tundra meadows. Through these encounters, my respect and admiration for bears— and their world—has continued to grow. I've also been lucky enough to meet several of Alaska's foremost bear researchers. The knowledge they've imparted to me, I now share with you, in this guide to Alaska's bears and the wild country they inhabit. ∎

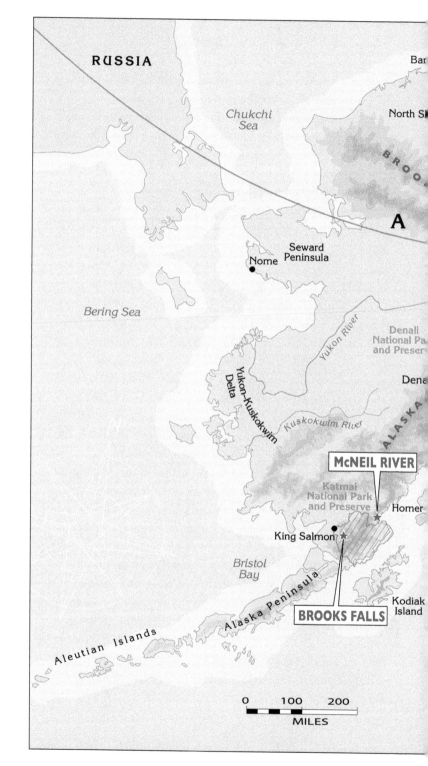

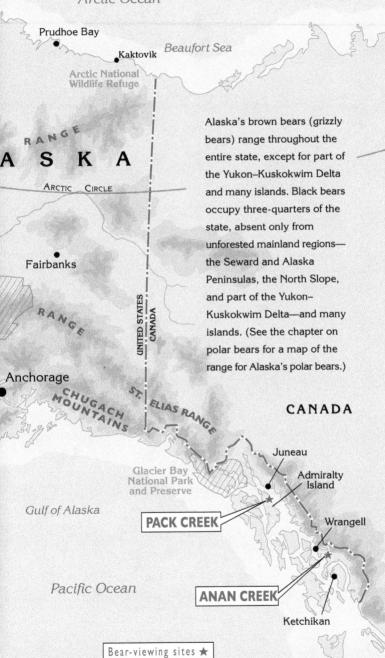

Arctic Ocean

Prudhoe Bay

Beaufort Sea

Kaktovik

Arctic National
Wildlife Refuge

RANGE

A S K A

ARCTIC CIRCLE

Fairbanks

RANGE

UNITED STATES

CANADA

Anchorage

CHUGACH
MOUNTAINS

ST. ELIAS RANGE

CANADA

Juneau

Glacier Bay
National Park
and Preserve

Admiralty
Island

Gulf of Alaska

PACK CREEK

Wrangell

Pacific Ocean

ANAN CREEK

Ketchikan

Bear-viewing sites ★

Alaska's brown bears (grizzly bears) range throughout the entire state, except for part of the Yukon–Kuskokwim Delta and many islands. Black bears occupy three-quarters of the state, absent only from unforested mainland regions—the Seward and Alaska Peninsulas, the North Slope, and part of the Yukon–Kuskokwim Delta—and many islands. (See the chapter on polar bears for a map of the range for Alaska's polar bears.)

THE POLAR BEAR

The polar bear's dense, double-layer fur keeps the animal well insulated during Arctic blizzards.

I t's strange, at first, to think of any bear as a marine mammal. But the more you learn about the polar bear and its lifestyle, the more you understand why biologists have placed it in a group that includes whales, seals, sea otters, and walrus.

The polar bear's life is so intimately tied to marine environments that some call it the sea bear; even its scientific name, *Ursus maritimus*, recognizes this connection. Others call it the ice bear, the lord of the Arctic. These too fit. Of all the earth's bears, only the polar bear lives exclusively in the Arctic. To be more precise, it is most at home on the Arctic's frozen seas. This is a world that for much of the year is dark and frigid, with icy winds, subzero temperatures, and fierce blizzards. Yet it's here that the polar bear flourishes. As Canadian researcher Ian Stirling puts it: "For thousands of years, the climate, the ice, and the seals upon which it feeds have shaped and finely tuned the evolution of this predator so exquisitely that it has become not just a symbol but the very embodiment of life in the Arctic."

Exactly how the polar bear adapted to the sea-ice environment is still something of a mystery. The species is believed to be a young one, somewhere between 300,000 and 500,000 years old (the age is still being debated). It's generally accepted that polar bears evolved from the brown bear line, perhaps along the Siberian coast. This might have happened during the Pleistocene ice age when a population of brown bears became isolated by an advancing glacial sheet. Secluded in an environment filled with seals and no other predatory competitors, these opportunistic feeders discovered a wide-open niche.

The idea of brown bears venturing onto sea ice and learning to hunt seals is not far-fetched. We know that brown bears now and then feed on seal carcasses and take seals that haul out on land. They've occasionally been seen along the Arctic Ocean's edge, sometimes while intermingling with polar bears while feeding on whale carcasses, and other times not far from basking seals; a few have even been spotted on the sea ice itself, up to 35 miles from land. Given this present-day behavior and the fact that bears are fast learners, it's easy to imagine an isolated group of brown bears gradually adapting to life as seal hunters.

They were successful enough to eventually produce the modern polar bear. Adult male polar bears may weigh up to 1,700 pounds and, standing on their hind legs, reach more than 11 feet high; more commonly, they weigh around 1,000 pounds. Adult females are considerably smaller, rarely weighing more than 600 to 700 pounds.

As generations of sea bears adapted to their new environment and life as a pure carnivore, their bodies went through a dramatic transformation. Most noticeably, their fur became hollow and translucent; the manner in which the hairs reflect light gives the fur a creamy white appearance, to better blend with snow and ice. And claws that had been long and straight for digging became shorter, sharper, and strongly curved, to permit a better grip on ice and prey.

More differences from the brown bears: instead of a wide, dish-faced head, polar bears have a long, narrower head with a Roman nose. And they have a much longer neck, which may help them keep their head above water when swimming. Another Arctic adaptation is their huge oar-like feet. Combined with partial webbing between the toes, these feet improve the polar bear's swimming ability. And on thin ice, the feet act much like snowshoes, enabling bears to cross ice that even a human might break through. On especially weak ice, the bear may spread its legs as wide as possible and crawl on its belly.

Polar bears don't slip on ice, because their footpads are covered with tiny nipple-like projections that increase friction between foot and ice. Also, the soles of their feet have small depressions that may act as suction cups to further improve the bears' grip as they run. Finally, the bottoms of their feet are heavily furred between the toes, which both aids in traction and insulates from the cold.

In contrast with their big feet, polar bears have tiny ears and tails. In that respect they follow a scientific rule-of-thumb that the farther north an animal lives, the smaller its extremities, to conserve body heat.

Polar bears are enthusiastic swimmers. They swim by moving their front paws in dog-paddle strokes, while hind legs help in diving, turning, and other maneuvering. Young bears especially seem to love swimming; but newborn cubs, which have little fat, cannot remain in cold Arctic waters for long or they'll become hypothermic. The thick, dense, fatty layer benefits older bears in two ways: it helps keep them warm and provides increased buoyancy. The abilities of even the most accomplished swimmers are being put to the test by diminishing sea ice, a major change in the polar bear's world that's connected to climate change.

While the fatty layer performs admirably in frigid water and subzero cold, it creates problems when temperatures warm in sum-

Polar bears sometimes sprawl on the ice or snow to keep from overheating.

mer or when a bear exercises hard: polar bears quickly overheat. To regulate body temperature, they (like other bears) have evolved "hot spots" on their face, footpads, inner thighs, and shoulder muscles to dissipate excess heat. To assist this heat loss, bears lie on their back, exposing legs, belly, and feet to the air. Swimming, eating snow, and panting are other ways they cool down. In summer they molt and spend more time resting.

For all their differences, brown bears and polar bears remain enough alike genetically that they can interbreed and produce fertile offspring. Hybrid cubs—produced in captivity—tend to be white at birth and most closely resemble their polar bear parent, but their fur may become bluish brown or yellowish white with age. Though hybrids are rare in the wild, such bears have been found. Sometimes called "grolar bears" or "pizzlies" (among other informal names) their mixed-species origins have been confirmed by genetic testing. One such bear killed by a hunter in the Canadian Arctic was predominantly white, but had brown patches and the long claws, concave face, and humped back characteristic of grizzlies.

Polar Bears and Climate Warming

Given their dependence on sea ice and ringed seals, it should come as no surprise that polar bears face a dire future if the Earth's atmosphere continues to warm. Based on evidence that stretches back to the 1980s, scientists who study the polar bear have reached a consensus that if the climate continues to warm and reduce Arctic sea ice as their models predict, "polar bears will largely disappear from the southern portions of their range by mid-century," including the Beaufort Sea, off Alaska's northern coast. And though populations of *Ursus maritimus* may persist in northern parts of its range, the species' "long-term viability . . . is uncertain." Those are the conclusions that Canadian researchers Ian Stirling and Andrew Derocher reach in their 2012 paper, "Effects of Climate Warming on Polar Bears: A Review of the Evidence," published in *Global Change Biology*.

The scientific evidence is overwhelming: not only is the Earth's climate heating up to an alarming degree (largely because of human activities), its effects are especially extreme in the Arctic; and the most visible consequence, over the past three decades, has been the rapid loss of sea ice—the polar bear's principle domain.

Both the increased seasonal melt of sea ice and extended ice-free periods harm the species, because of the bears' dependency on stable ice platforms to hunt ringed seals in spring and early summer.

Diminished access to their primary prey, especially during the critical seal pupping season, results in "longer periods of fasting, lower body condition, decreased access to denning areas, fewer and smaller cubs, lower survival of cubs, as well as bears of other age classes, and, finally, subpopulation decline toward eventual extirpation."

If the climate continues to warm, Stirling and Derocher warn, polar bears are likely to disappear from southern parts of their range within three to four decades. Another scientist, Steve Amstrup, has predicted that up to two-thirds of the world's polar bears could die off by the mid-21st century.

While polar bears have survived other warming periods, the circumstances of this one are much different, given several other "stressors" such as a human presence throughout much of the Arctic (which increases bear-human conflicts), industrial activities, chemical contaminants in the food chain, and reduced prey populations. In short, Stirling and Derocher write, the combination of these factors with climate warming poses "a profound threat to polar bear survival."

The 2012 "review of the evidence" was followed by another discouraging report issued in 2015 by the US Geological Survey, which conducts polar bear research. The authors of "Evaluating and Ranking Threats to the Long-Term Persistence of Polar Bears," found that declining sea-ice conditions and the polar bear's primary prey remain the species' chief threats. Using new information on both actual and predicted sea-ice losses and polar bear responses to changed circumstances, the authors concluded that the outlook for polar bears "worsened over time through the end of the century," whether greenhouse gas emissions were stabilized or continued unabated, though reduced emissions would lessen the damage. Ultimately, it appears that the "long-term persistence"—that is, survival—of polar bears depends on stabilized sea ice habitat.

If Arctic waters eventually become ice free as some scientific models predict, the sea bear may be doomed. ■

Large cracks in the ice, called leads, attract polar bears hunting seals resting on the ice or swimming in the open water.

Hoping for a meal, a polar bear inspects a seal lair.

HOME ON THE ICE

Polar bears are scattered throughout the Northern Hemisphere's region of ice-covered seas, inhabiting the lands and frozen waters of Canada, Greenland, Norway, Russia, and the United States. The best current population estimate is between 20,000 and 25,000 animals.

Until the 1960s, polar bears were believed to be circumpolar nomads that wandered randomly through the Arctic. But close monitoring has radically altered that view. It turns out that polar bears have a seasonal fidelity to certain regions: at any given season, an individual bear is likely to be found in the same area from one year to the next. Exactly how they navigate remains unknown, though it's suspected they may use the position of the sun or stars, or even the earth's magnetic field. With the exception of females raising their cubs, they travel the ice pack alone.

Now, instead of a single circumpolar population, scientists divide polar bears into 19 subpopulations. Alaska's bears form two distinct subpopulations, though there is some intermingling; not so long ago their combined numbers were estimated to be 3,000 to 5,000 animals, but more recently researchers and managers have concluded the population size is "unknown." About 900 live on the southern Beaufort Sea ice pack, and their numbers have been declining; the rest range through the Chukchi and Bering Seas, spending about two-thirds of their time in Russian territory.

The Beaufort population occupies an area of 360,000 square miles off Alaska's northern coast. These bears are long-distance travelers—moving anywhere from 880 to 3,800 miles a year, according to researchers who tracked more than 100 females for a dozen years. (The females were fitted with radio collars and tracked by satellite telemetry. Males weren't followed because, with necks larger than their heads, traditional collars fell off. Since 2010, researchers have applied glue-on satellite tags to males, but they last only a couple of months and don't provide year-round data.) Single females tended to cover more ground than females constrained by cubs.

The home ranges of individual Beaufort bears varied from 4,900 to as many as 230,000 square miles, an area nearly the size of Texas. Each bear's range overlaps with the ranges of other bears. And because of shifting sea ice and changes in the availability of food, a range's size and shape varies from year to year.

Because polar bears prefer the edges of active ice, where food is most easily accessible, their travel is closely tied to seasonal movements of the ice pack. Beaufort bears move north in the summer and south in the winter as they follow the ice-pack edge, which retreats during the warmer months and then advances as the weather cools. It's intriguing that many of these bears also show an east-west movement, which likely reflects seasonal changes in the distribution of sea ice and open water, changes connected to regional ocean currents.

In the Chukchi and Bering Seas off Western Alaska, the ice pack's leading edge moves nearly 900 miles in a normal year. To stay

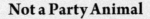

Not a Party Animal

Polar bears are generally considered solitary creatures. They rarely engage in social interaction besides mating. (The relationship of a female with her cubs is an obvious exception.) But there are times and places where polar bears gather in large groups and, though infrequently, even show signs of playing.

An abundance of food, for instance a whale carcass, will sometimes draw crowds of bears. A bowhead whale carcass drifting between the pack ice off Norway attracted 56 polar bears. Here in Alaska, both beached whales and the remains of bowheads harvested by the residents of Iñupiat communities may lure dozens of bears.

Seasonal movement patterns may also bring bears together. In the Hudson's Bay region of Canada, the particular pattern of ice-pack melting results in the unusual phenomenon of large numbers of polar bears spending summers on land. Once fall arrives, they gather at points along the coast to wait for the sea ice to form. The most famous of those points is Cape Churchill in Manitoba, where 50 or more polar bears have been counted at a single time along a 1¼-mile-long sand spit. Churchill's bears are a major attraction, drawing thousands of visitors each year. Both young and mature bears have been seen playing there. Sometimes they roll and wres-

on the edge, this region's bears have been known to travel from 1,800 to 3,000 miles a year. Radio-tracking data indicates an average home range for Western Alaska polar bears of 96,000 square miles, the largest in the world and more than twice the average for Beaufort Sea bears. And while Beaufort bears show major east-west movement, Western Alaska bears move mostly north and south.

Polar bears prefer to remain on sea ice year-round, if possible, because it's there they find their favorite food: seals. They're most drawn to sea ice adjacent to mainland coastlines and island archipelagos, where biological productivity is high and seals are most abun-

tle on the ground; at other times they stand and push or slap each other in the shoulders and chest.

Changing patterns in the southern Beaufort Sea have led to a less famous gathering of polar bears in Alaska, but one that's increasingly popular with wildlife viewers and photographers from around the world. It's estimated that about 10 percent—or about 100—of the Beaufort bears now annually come ashore. Of those, a third or more congregate near the coastal village of Kaktovik each September and October, to feed on the remains of whales taken by Iñupiat subsistence hunters.

While impressive, neither the Churchill nor Kaktovik gatherings compare with what Henry Elliott described in a government report in the late 19th century, while recounting a remarkable encounter with polar bears on Alaska's St. Matthew Island in August 1874: "[W]e met bears—yea, hundreds of them. . . . Their white forms in the distance always answered to our search, though they ran from our immediate presence with the greatest celerity. . . their paths were broad and well beaten all over the island. We could not have observed less than 250 or 300 of these animals while we were there." By 1900, however, the bears' numbers on St. Matthew had dropped to near zero, apparently because of intense hunting. ∎

dant. The ice, affected by both ocean currents and winds, frequently cracks and refreezes. The result is a diverse environment that includes open-water leads and thin ice through which seals can easily create their breathing holes—the openings through the ice that give them entry to the sea and a place where they can surface to breathe.

The open-water leads, long and narrow, may extend for hundreds of miles and stay open even in subzero cold. They commonly form where the shifting pack ice and more stable shore-fast ice meet. Areas of open water that are more rounded and pond-like also form.

Fascinating Fur

The polar bear's fur is in two layers: a dense, wool-like under-layer and a more open layer of longer guard hairs.

The hair can take on a number of shades, because the outer guard hairs are not white, but hollow and colorless. The fur looks white largely because of the way it scatters light. A bear that appears white at midday may have a bluish cast to its fur in early morning and then look yellow in the waning light of evening. And if the bear appears darker in high winds, it's because you're seeing glimpses of its black skin as hair is blown aside.

The hollow nature of the outer hairs helps to maximize their insulating ability. Research reported in 2015 further explained that the hollow hairs have complex structures of "membrane pores," which make the hairs better insulators than simple tubes.

The bear's two-layer fur works well when dry but has little insulating value when wet. What keeps a polar bear from becoming chilled while swimming in Arctic waters is still being studied by researchers; the bear's dense layer of fat plays some role, but it's likely other mechanisms also contribute. The hard, hollow guard hairs shed water easily. To dry off after leaving water, bears need only shake themselves vigorously as they emerge from a swim, sometimes rolling in the snow to aid the drying process. ■

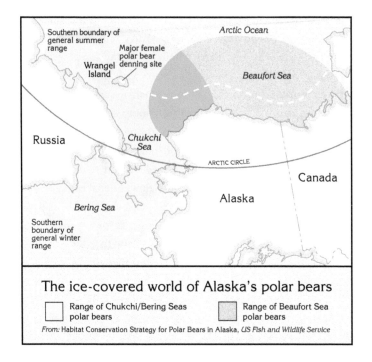

Southern boundary of general summer range

Major female polar bear denning site

Wrangel Island

Arctic Ocean

Beaufort Sea

Russia

Chukchi Sea

ARCTIC CIRCLE

Canada

Alaska

Bering Sea

Southern boundary of general winter range

The ice-covered world of Alaska's polar bears

Range of Chukchi/Bering Seas polar bears

Range of Beaufort Sea polar bears

From: Habitat Conservation Strategy for Polar Bears in Alaska, *US Fish and Wildlife Service*

Known as polynyas, some are the size of a football field; others cover hundreds of square miles. Like many leads, some polynyas survive even the coldest weather. Although they may vary in size from year to year, these recurring polynyas tend to remain in about the same spot and are critically important feeding areas for many marine species, including polar bears.

A DIET OF SEALS

Ringed seals make up the bulk of the polar bear diet. One of the smallest of their kind, ringed seals at maturity average 130 to 150 pounds. Though adults have dark fur, females give birth to pups with white coats, which camouflage the defenseless young. They are born in April, in snow-covered lairs, or cavities, which incorporate breathing holes in the ice.

Polar bears locate the hidden lairs by smell. While their hearing abilities have been described as "sensitive" and their eyesight is roughly the same as a human's (though adaptations prevent snow blindness), polar bears are largely dependent on a sense of smell that's extraordinary—enabling it to smell a seal's snow-covered breathing hole from as much as a mile away. (Some people claim polar bears can detect rotting carcasses a hundred miles away.)

Approaching a lair slowly and quietly, the bear apparently places itself directly over the breathing hole and stands absolutely still until it either hears or smells a seal below. Then it raises up on its hind legs and crashes down with its front paws. If the bear breaks through the snow roof on the first try, it grabs for a meal; if not, it may jump on the roof several more times, or dig through it. By then, of course, the seal has usually disappeared through the breathing hole, into the sea.

While polar bears must seek out hidden lairs in winter and early spring, hunting is easier in summer, when breathing holes are exposed and seals can often be found basking on the ice. To catch their prey, the bears have perfected the arts of stalking and still-hunting.

When a bear spots a seal on the ice, it stops and remains motionless, sometimes for several minutes, as if figuring out the best way to get close. Lowering its head, the bear then walks slowly and steadily toward the seal, sometimes moving into a semi-crouched position as it gets close. When it's within 50 to 100 feet, the bear charges, while the stunned seal tries to escape through its hole into the sea.

Though stalks are more dramatic, polar bears more often use still-hunting techniques. They position themselves beside a breathing hole or on the edge of an open-water lead and wait for a seal to surface. They usually lie on their stomach and chest, though some bears prefer to sit or stand. It's essential the bear make no noise because sound is easily transmitted through snow-covered ice. When a seal finally surfaces to breathe, the bear pounces. Biting it on

The Walrus Connection

Adult male walrus—weighing up to two tons and wielding long ivory tusks—are among the few animals capable of killing mature polar bears. Yet polar bears will sometimes risk injury to prey on walrus young or, more rarely, adults.

In *Wild Life Beyond the North*, author Frank Illingworth recounts a polar bear–walrus battle described by an earlier Arctic explorer: "The bear crept forward with the utmost care, making for the smallest of three animals lying at the edge of the water close under the sleepy eyes of an old bull. As the bear made its final sally the bull turned to the defence of its smaller companion. . . . in a matter of seconds the bear lay bleeding from a mortal wound and the old bull, roaring angrily, lifted itself on its foreflippers and surveyed the scene of its victory before taking to the water."

Anthropologist and writer Richard Nelson was told by Kavik, an Iñupiat hunter in Wainwright, Alaska, of a polar bear that tried to get a baby walrus from a herd. "Kavik said that they saw the bear pick up a chunk (or several chunks) of ice with both paws, stand up on its hind legs and throw it at the walruses in a vain attempt to move the large ones away from the infant." ■

the head or upper body, the bear flips the seal onto the ice; it then bites the seal's head and neck a few more times and drags it several yards from the water before eating it.

The bear first devours the fatty layer; then, if still hungry, it may eat some meat. The preference is understandable: most of the calories are in the fat, and a polar bear is able to assimilate 97 percent of the fat it ingests.

Polar bears miss their prey far more often than they kill it, averaging about one seal every four or five days. Thus they've had to adapt to a feast-or-famine diet—and a life of constant hunting. They also eat other foods when circumstances allow. They've been seen preying on other seals, beluga whales, walrus, musk oxen, hares, lemmings, ground squirrels, waterfowl, fish, crabs, clams—even other polar bears. They also scavenge the carcasses of whales and other marine mammals; their feeding on the remains of human-killed whales near the Iñupiat village of Kaktovik, along Alaska's Arctic coast, in fall and early winter, has made this the best place to see Alaska's polar bears. When meat isn't readily available, they've been known to eat bird eggs, kelp, grasses, and berries, though such foods don't provide nearly as much sustenance as their normal diet.

MOTHERS AND THEIR DENS

Unlike Alaska's brown and black bears, most polar bears do not spend their winters in hibernation, because ringed seals provide a reliable year-round supply of food. While any polar bear may build a temporary den to escape extreme cold or Arctic storms—when wind-chill temperatures can drop below –100°F—scientists tell us that only pregnant females normally den for extended periods, though some Alaska Natives disagree with this view.

In Alaska, female polar bears normally begin breeding in their fifth year, mating on the sea ice in April or May over a period of several days after they've been tracked and courted by males. Like brown and black bears, the female polar bears don't release eggs for fertilization until stimulated by the physical act of mating. Impregnated females begin storing fat to get themselves and their cubs-to-be through the next winter; by some estimates, they must gain at least 200 pounds before entering their dens. In one extreme case, a female captured in Canada increased her weight from 214 to 1,112 pounds over a nine-month period.

In most Arctic regions, female bears leave the sea ice and come ashore to den between September and November. Most choose sites within 10 miles of the coast, but some have been found 75 miles inland. The females tunnel into snowbanks and build oval chambers. These snow dens are excellent insulators, with the difference between inside and outside temperatures as much as 60°F.

Though they can den wherever there are snowdrifts, pregnant females often concentrate in certain core areas. Such maternity denning areas have been identified in Canada, Greenland, Norway, and Russia. One of the most famous is Wrangel Island, a mountainous, 60-mile-long landform off Russia's northeastern coast. Hundreds of females den here annually, including up to 80 percent of Western Alaska's breeding population.

Farther to the east, Alaska's Beaufort Sea population has proven to be exceptional in that many female bears build dens on sea ice instead of land. Of 90 maternity dens found by polar bear researcher Steve Amstrup between 1981 and 1991, more than half were on sea ice, some as far as 500 miles offshore—a startling dis-

Polar bear cubs rely on their mothers for survival and protection.

When Polar Pears and Humans Meet

Because they are the Arctic's largest terrestrial carnivores and foremost predators, polar bears always prompt discussion of the dangers they pose to humans. Polar bears, it is commonly asserted, are the only bears that regularly stalk people and treat them as prey. Most Native communities in northwestern Alaska will kill or drive away a polar bear that approaches too closely, because it's considered dangerous. Yet while living with the Iñupiat Eskimos, anthropologist Richard Nelson was told by hunters that "a bear will usually run away if it sees a man."

While there are many accounts of polar bears stalking people, biologists believe their approach is often triggered by simple curiosity. Another fact to consider: a human is about the same size as a ringed seal. Polar bears, in at least some instances, may mistake a human for a seal. One way that Iñupiats have traditionally hunted polar bears is to "play seal," hoping the animal will stalk them.

An analysis of polar bear attacks in Canada between 1965 and 1985 suggests that the adult males stalked humans much as they

covery because it had always been assumed that polar bears den exclusively on land, where they escape the danger of having a den crushed, flooded, or broken apart by shifting sea ice. More recent data indicates about 40 percent den on sea ice, a drop that likely reflects diminished stable sea ice, tied to climate change.

Amstrup suspects that land dens were more common until the early 1900s, when increased hunting with firearms by whalers and Iñupiat Eskimos killed off the land-denning females or greatly reduced their numbers. Late in the 20th century, Alaska's Native residents voluntarily decreased their kill of female bears, which may account for a resurgence of maternity land denning along the Beaufort Sea. One preferred area is the Arctic National Wildlife Refuge's coastal plain, a political battleground between people who

would a seal. In nearly every case, the bear had to be killed to end the assault. Often thin or old, some were likely starving animals; others may have been adolescent males that hadn't fine-tuned their hunting skills. Females that assaulted humans usually had cubs and in most cases called off the attack themselves, which suggests they were behaving defensively.

Despite the polar bear's reputation as a dangerous animal, documented accounts of their assaults on people are rare. Research wildlife ecologist Tom Smith has verified only three fatal attacks in Alaska since 1883 (with six more in Canada).

The bottom line, according to polar bear biologist Steve Amstrup: "Polar bears must be respected because of their size, speed, and strength. When in the bear's world, humans must take extreme care to stay out of their way."

The truth, of course, is that humans have been much more deadly to bears than the other way around. One researcher estimated our species has killed more than 100,000 polar bears since the start of the 18th century. ■

would like to preserve it as wilderness and others who want it opened to oil and gas development.

Settled in their dens, hibernating females give birth in December or January, usually to a pair of cubs. The newborns weigh 1 to 1½ pounds, have such fine hair that they may appear hairless, and are blind. The mother nurses her young on cream-like milk that can be up to 36 percent fat, with more than three times the energy content of either human's or cow's milk. It also contains the proteins and carbohydrates needed by developing cubs to grow quickly. When they emerge from dens in March or April, the cubs weigh 20 to 30 pounds; by their first birthday, they'll weigh up to 200 pounds.

The young bears will stay with their mom for about 28 months as they learn how to hunt seals and survive on the sea ice.

Hide and Seek

One of the most intriguing stories about polar bears is that they cover their black nose when hunting seals. Some Arctic explorers and Native residents have reported seeing polar bears use their tongue or paws to hide their nose when stalking their next meal. Some say the bear might even push a chunk of ice ahead of its nose or pack snow around it to conceal the only part of its body not camouflaged by white fur. Polar bear biologists don't completely discredit this legendary behavior, though most remain skeptical. ■

Between 20 and 40 percent die their first year; some are killed by other polar bears, but this is considered rare. They are much more likely to starve, be killed by humans, or freeze to death. The hardest times, however, are those first few years after weaning, when bears must adapt to life on their own, and adolescents suffer the highest mortality.

Unless all of a female's cubs die before weaning, at least 3 years will pass between litters. Given that few polar bears live beyond 20 years in the wild, most females have five litters or less in their lifetime.

FUTURE OF THE POLAR BEAR

Indigenous peoples have hunted polar bears for as long as the two have shared the Arctic. Yet in hunting and killing *nanuq*, they traditionally treated the ice bear with great respect: there were strict rules of conduct to be followed when hunting the bear and after its death. The polar bear was killed not only for its fur and meat, but also as a rite of initiation, to test the courage of boys making the passage to manhood.

An ally of Native shamans, the polar bear was believed to have a powerful spirit. It played a central role in many religious ceremonies, creation legends, and other myths. Some of the rituals are still practiced, stories are still told. But in an era when firearms and snowmachines have replaced lances and dog teams, the polar bear has lost much of its power and place of reverence among Alaska's Iñupiat peoples.

European-American explorers, fur traders, whalers, and sport hunters commonly showed polar bears little or none of the respect given by Native residents, at least partly because firearms made it possible to kill them in large numbers from afar. Early visitors to the Arctic often killed any polar bears they saw. In Canada's Amundsen Gulf in 1896, a whaling captain shot 35 polar bears for sport in a single afternoon. Explorer and author Vilhjalmur Stefansson displayed the casual, almost indifferent, attitude that led to the slaughter of

A female polar bear with cub searches for scents on the ice.

polar bears: "I have killed many dozens of polar bears. . . . the risk to men in hunting them is commonly overrated."

The nature of the hunt changed dramatically in the 1940s with the use of ski planes. Trophy hunters from around the world hired planes to fly them across the ice pack, looking for bears. Pilots would often work in tandem: when a polar bear was spotted, one would drop a hunter on the ice while the other herded the bear within shooting range. Worldwide, the reported annual kill in the mid-1960s was 1,300 animals.

Concern over the polar bear slaughter led to a 1965 international meeting of the United States, Canada, Greenland, Norway, and the Soviet Union, resulting in a 1973 agreement that sets limits on the killing and capturing of polar bears and instructs each country to protect polar bear ecosystems. The United States went on to prohibit all hunting of polar bears except for Native subsistence, specifically banning aerial hunting—but giving no special protection to bears in dens or to females with cubs. In 1988 a landmark agreement signed by the Iñupiat of Alaska's North Slope and by northwestern Canada's Inuvialuit people included a voluntary limit on their kill of females and cubs in the Beaufort Sea region.

As recently as the late 1990s, Alaska's polar bear population was considered to be healthy and stable, perhaps even slightly increasing, but its status changed dramatically over the following 15 to 20 years. The southern Beaufort Sea population is now considered to be declining. The status for the Chukchi-Bering Seas population is unknown, but researchers who studied the bears reported in 2014 that they appeared to be in good condition and the addition of cubs into the population (known as "recruitment") remained high. While overhunting and Arctic development were once considered the species' primary threats, the consensus now is that climate change and associated declines in Arctic sea ice present the greatest danger. In 2008, the US government officially listed polar bears as globally "threatened" under the Endangered Species Act because of ongoing and forecasted declines in the sea ice upon which the species is so dependent.

The United States is the only Arctic nation that has not set aside some sort of polar bear sanctuary. The coastal plain of the Arctic National Wildlife Refuge has been serving that purpose, but it never was officially protected as wilderness, and Congress could still open it to development.

One thing seems certain: the polar bear's fate is tied to our species' actions, including—and especially—the ongoing use of fossil fuels that is the primary cause of the current climate change crisis. No longer is it sufficient that we leave vast areas of the circumpolar region in a pristine state. Now governments, businesses, and individuals around the world must change their behaviors for *pisugtooq* ("the great traveler") to thrive or perhaps even survive. ■

THE BROWN BEAR AND GRIZZLY BEAR

A brown bear approaches a Kodiak stream where other bears fish,
avoiding a large male dominating the best fishing site.

O ne North American animal, above all others, has come to
symbolize wilderness and raw animal power: the brown
bear, also known as the grizzly. This is an animal that
commands our respect when we travel through its wild, ever-
shrinking world.

In the distant past, the brown bear's world was a vast one.
These bears once roamed through most of Europe and Asia and even
occupied a slice of northern Africa. The earliest brown bear fossils,
found in China, have been dated at 500,000 years old, and the species itself may go back a million or more years.

The ancestors of modern brown bears apparently migrated from northeast Asia to Alaska along the same Bering Land Bridge taken by the ancestors of Native Americans during the Pleistocene ice age. The bears came in two or more distinct pulses, between 50,000 and 10,000 years ago, and spread throughout much of North America. They once ranged from Northern Alaska and Western Canada south to Mexico, and from the West Coast east across the Great Plains of the United States.

As recently as 1850, an estimated 50,000 to 100,000 brown/grizzly bears inhabited the Lower 48 states. But their range receded and their numbers rapidly declined as they came in contact—and conflict—with European and American explorers and developers. Now about 1,500 remain in the Lower 48. To the north, Canada is home to some 15,000 to 20,000 members of the species *Ursus arctos*. But the great bear's primary North American enclave is Alaska, where an estimated 31,000 live.

The bears occupy nearly the entire state, except for part of the Yukon–Kuskokwim Delta and numerous islands. They inhabit almost every northern ecosystem imaginable, from coastal rain forests to Interior woodlands, high alpine meadows, and Arctic tundra. It's no wonder that Alaska is often called the last stronghold of North America's brown bears: this is where they've been given their last, best chance to survive. And even thrive.

As its historic range shows, the brown bear is a remarkably adaptable creature. What especially set it apart from other bears was the species' ability to adapt to the immense open landscapes left by glaciation. Over time, the brown bear developed the tools necessary for tundra life: long claws and powerful neck and back muscles to make it easier to dig plant roots and rodents from the earth, with a large body and aggressive nature to help the bear defend itself—and a female defend her young—in open spaces.

Brown bears and grizzlies are essentially the same animal, although the larger, coastal members of *Ursus arctos* are usually referred to as brown bears and the smaller bears of Interior Alaska

Bears, like humans, can comfortably stand on two feet.

are called grizzlies. Whether they are labeled browns or grizzlies, the bears have a distinctive body shape characterized by a large shoulder hump, unusually long claws, and a wide, massive head that is concave in profile and frequently described as dish-faced. The body has variously been termed chunky, massive, or sturdy, but browns and grizzlies are anything but clumsy. Or slow. They've been clocked at speeds of up to 40 miles per hour over short distances—fast enough to catch a horse.

Their fur comes in many colors: brown, cinnamon, red, blond, and even black, or a blend of various shades. Many Interior residents have hairs with silvery or frosted tips, which gives their fur a grizzled appearance—hence the name.

Like humans, browns and grizzlies (and other bears) can comfortably stand on two feet. They sometimes do this to see or smell better, feed, engage in play, or fight. But it is not a sign that they're about to attack, as commonly portrayed on magazine covers. Also contrary to popular belief, younger members of the species are excellent climbers, and even adults can pull themselves several yards up a tree if the branches are sturdy enough.

As with many mammals, females tend to live longer than males. Biologists have documented females 30 and older, though a sow in her early to mid-20s is an old bear. Males rarely reach their 20s; one possible reason is that males are frequently injured in fights during the mating season, and over the years these injuries take their toll.

Browns and grizzlies, like other bears, have excellent hearing and a superior sense of smell. And their eyesight is quite good, despite the common belief that they have poor vision. The species is considered highly intelligent, in the sense that the bears are able to adapt to a wide range of circumstances and seem capable of "thinking through" problems—for instance, how to reach human food that's been cached in a tree.

SURVIVING WINTER

Among the most fascinating of bear adaptations is winter denning, a strategy that enables the animal to survive prolonged periods of harsh weather and reduced food. Over the millennia, denning has proved to be a great way for northern bears to spend the winter.

The time at which brown bears enter and leave their dens varies considerably throughout Alaska, but certain generalities apply.

Native Respect

Indigenous peoples have traditionally regarded the brown bear with a mixture of fear and respect. In *The Sacred Paw*, authors Paul Shepard and Barry Sanders write, "From time far older than memory, the bear has been a special being: human-like, yet close to the animals and hence to the source of life." Native tribes throughout North America traditionally believed the grizzly to be half human, or that humans were descended from bears.

In Alaska, to cite one example, the Athabascan residents of Huslia and Hughes have traditionally shown an "unparalleled feeling of awe toward brown bears," cultural anthropologist Richard Nelson wrote in *Make Prayers to the Raven: A Koyukon View of the Northern Forest*, based on the years that he lived in those northern Alaska Interior villages. When Koyukon men hunted, they would follow prescribed rituals. Never should a man brag about hunting a brown bear. And if one is killed, its meat is to be left outside the village for a time, to allow the animal's spiritual energy to depart. The meat is finally shared in a ritual feast that honors the bear's spirit.

Alaska's other Native peoples have historically exhibited similar attitudes. Alutiiq residents of the Alaska Peninsula believed that bears are human ancestors that must be shown respect. Boys being initiated into the hunt would cleanse themselves the night before by taking a sweat bath while an elder chanted. Upon killing his first brown bear, a boy was to put his hand down its throat to remove his fear of the bear and become strong. The hunt would culminate with a ceremonial feast, with bones returned to the kill site, again as a sign of respect.

In contemporary times, many such traditions have been forgotten or ignored. As one hunter told anthropologists Jim Fall and Lisa Hutchinson: "The way I was brought up, we got to respect the bear. But nowadays, it's starting to change. They [some other hunters] don't care what happens to the bear after it's dead. . . . But me and my brothers still do the things to the animals that we were taught to do. I don't see no other way." ∎

Pregnant females are the first to den and, accompanied by newborn cubs, the last to leave their winter shelters, while adult males are the last to den and first to emerge.

At one end of the denning spectrum is Kodiak Island, where adult males may not hibernate at all if the winter weather is relatively mild, snow is scarce, and food can be found. While Kodiak's males vary their winter pattern, pregnant females—more dependent on the security of den sites—are more predictable. They usually enter dens by early November and stay there until late May or even June.

At the other extreme is Alaska's Arctic, where pregnant females spend up to eight months in dens, from mid-September to late May. Males more typically enter dens in mid-October and leave by mid-May.

In the coldest regions, where midwinter temperatures may fall to -60°F, the bears often choose sites where snow builds up, adding insulation for the dens beneath the ground. The timing of denning in these regions may be tied to the season's first heavy snowfall.

Browns and grizzlies most commonly dig their own dens in the earth, usually on moderate to steep slopes. A den is often prepared weeks before the bear goes into hibernation. The underground shelters are built to size for the most efficient use of body heat and may consist of both an entry tunnel and a denning chamber. Some bears add nests of grass, willow, or whatever plants are available.

Alaska Range grizzlies usually dig fairly shallow dens, with roofs 6 inches to a foot thick. Facing almost any direction, they are built at a wide range of elevations, from riverbanks to high mountain slopes. Frequently they're dug among clumps of willows, perhaps for the stability that roots provide.

In Southeast Alaska, meanwhile, brown bears prefer old-growth forest; sites are commonly excavated under live trees or snags. Though dirt dens are preferred throughout most of Alaska, brown bears often use natural rock cavities on both Kodiak and Admiralty Islands, where milder winters make snow insulation less important.

Of Browns and Grizzlies

An Interior grizzly bear feeds on tundra berries; (right) a brown bear catches a red salmon in Brooks River, Katmai National Park.

What, exactly, is the difference between a brown bear and a grizzly bear? The distinction, it turns out, is a rather arbitrary one for these animals, which all belong to the species *Ursus arctos*. In general terms, brown bears are coastal animals, while members of the same species living in interior regions are known as grizzlies. The grizzlies tend to have longer claws and a bigger hump, be lighter in color, and have a more dish-shaped face than their coastal cousins. On average, they are also considerably smaller, mainly because brown bears have access to more plentiful energy-rich foods, especially salmon.

Adult female grizzlies on the North Slope average about 220 pounds in springtime, while those in the Alaska Range average closer to 280. By fall, adult bears often weigh up to 1½ times more than they did only four months earlier, so an adult female that weighs 260 pounds in May can tip the scales at 400 by the time it enters its winter den. A large male grizzly may weigh 400 to 500 pounds in spring and 600 to 700 just before denning.

And brown bears? Adult females average 400 to 500 pounds in early summer, sometimes reaching 600 to 700 in fall. Males, meanwhile, generally range from 500 to 900 pounds, with some giants reaching autumn weights of 1,500 pounds or more.

Coastal browns live in denser populations than grizzlies, again reflecting habitat and food differences. Kodiak and Admiralty Islands and the Katmai region of the Alaska Peninsula average about one bear per square mile. At the other extreme is the eastern Brooks Range, which can sustain only one grizzly for every 35 to 40 square miles.

Home ranges—the areas that meet all of an individual bear's requirements for food, shelter, mating, and denning—show similar variability. On Admiralty Island, for example, females have ranges that average 10 square miles, while on the North Slope they average 130 square miles. Males' home ranges are typically two to four times larger. (The home ranges of individual bears aren't exclusive territories, but overlap.) ■

Inside the den, bears enter a state of hibernation in which body temperatures and metabolic functions are only slightly reduced. They don't eat, drink, defecate, or urinate for long periods and survive by living off fat reserves.

LIFE AS A CUB

All of Alaska's brown and grizzly bears begin their lives in January or February, within protected dens. Pregnant females give birth to litters of one to four cubs, most commonly two. Blind, toothless, nearly hairless, and helpless, the newborns weigh a pound or less, small enough to fit into a human's cupped hands. The cubs begin nursing almost immediately and, nourished by rich milk, grow quickly.

Upon leaving their den in spring, cubs weigh about 15 pounds, give or take a few pounds; by autumn they may weigh 60 to 70 pounds. Because their young are highly vulnerable, females with newborn cubs usually spend their first weeks in out-of-the-way, protected places with good visibility, such as upper ridges.

Like other members of the species, a new mother emerging from her den goes through a transitional "walking hibernation" phase, characterized by lethargy and poor appetite, as she internally shifts gears from wintertime torpor to a highly active summertime mode. While it takes several days for Mom to work up an appetite, first-year cubs have frequent hunger pains and nurse every two to three hours.

Being new to the world and its myriad hazards, first-year cubs are absolutely dependent on their mother. When separated they may sniff out her location, noses held close to the ground, but visual and auditory signals are also crucial to their bonding process. For instance, females may use distress calls, such as a woofing sound, when separated from their cubs.

A separation between mother and young can, in rare instances, lead to temporary cub adoption. Such adoptions have been observed at Alaska's McNeil River State Game Sanctuary, where dozens of brown bears congregate each summer to feed on

An Alaska Peninsula brown bear and its first year cub. Spring cubs nurse frequently but also graze on new sedges and other plants.

salmon. Cubs that become separated from their mother occasionally join up with other family groups. The adoptions are usually brief, lasting from a few minutes to several hours. But in one documented case, a cub remained with its new family an entire season.

Adult bears, wolves, coyotes, and even eagles pose a threat to small brown and grizzly cubs. Up to 30 percent of first-year cubs die, with many killed (and sometimes eaten) by other brown/grizzly bears. For many years it was believed—or assumed—that only adult males kill cubs, but adult females have on rare occasions been observed killing cubs that belong to another family.

Cubs also face the danger of death from disease, malnutrition, and accidents like falls and drownings. Larger litters often have runts unable to compete with the rest; some die right in the den.

Cubs that survive their second year have a good chance of reaching adulthood. As the cubs grow, predators such as coyotes and eagles no longer pose a threat, though wolves and other bears remain a danger. The next major hurdle follows weaning, when adolescents are driven away to fend for themselves. Young brown bears are generally weaned during their third spring, at age 2½ . It appears there's a hormonal shift in the female related to the end of lactation, and she simply stops being a mom. Mortality rates are high for newly weaned cubs, but if they can make it to about 5 years of age, their mortality rate drops to 5 percent, until old age finally catches up to them.

Larry Aumiller, former longtime manager of the McNeil sanctuary, once watched as a female turned on her pair of 2½-year-old cubs. "All of a sudden, she lunged at them," he recalls. "They were really befuddled." Over the next two days, the female became increasingly aggressive, chasing the cubs and even biting them on the rump until they left. In less than a week, she went into estrus and mated.

Weaned siblings may remain together for a season or two, sometimes even denning together. But as they approach maturity, they inevitably part. Females tend to establish home ranges that overlap, or are adjacent to, their mother's. Males, however, are likely to wander far in search of new stomping grounds.

OPPORTUNISTIC OMNIVORES

Descended from carnivores, brown bears have evolved into opportunistic omnivores. John Muir once commented: "To him almost everything is food except granite." An exaggeration, but not far off the mark. The species eats an extremely wide variety of foods: everything from insects and berries to fish, carrion, and human garbage.

Bears consume enormous quantities of grass and sedges at certain times of year, but they'll also eagerly eat meat. Their taste for salmon is well documented and they prey on mammals when opportunities present themselves. Biologist Sterling Miller, who studied

Classifying the Browns

Because they vary so much in physical appearance, brown/ grizzly bears were once classified into hundreds of sub-species. In 1918, scientist C. H. Merriam identified more than 90 subspecies in North America alone. In 1963, biologist Bob Rausch offered a simplified classification that was widely accepted for decades: that all North American brown/grizzly bears belong to a single subspecies, *Ursus arctos horribilis*, with the exception of Kodiak Island browns, recognized as *Ursus arctos middendorffi*. Now even that distinction has largely been dropped.

Kodiak bears were for many years separated from other members of the species because their skulls tend to be wider, a little more massive, reflecting thousands of years of isolation from mainland populations. The Kodiak Archipelago was likely first populated with brown bears during one of the Pleistocene's glacial periods, when bears may have crossed an ice bridge to the island or perhaps ridden across Shelikof Strait on ice floes. However they got there, Kodiak's browns evolved into the continent's largest: males may weigh up to 1,500 or 1,600 pounds in fall.

Genetic work by Gerry Shields and Sandra Talbot in the 1990s raised questions about these subspecies distinctions. Their studies at the University of Alaska's Institute of Arctic Biology showed that Kodiak and mainland bears are similar enough genetically to be classified as the same subspecies and that's how things stand now. What's more, those studies reveal that brown bears on Southeast Alaska's Admiralty, Baranof, and Chichagof Islands—the ABC bears—are genetically distinct from all other Alaskan brown bears. Most intriguing of all, the research suggests that the ABC bears are genetically more closely linked to polar bears than to other brown bears. Still, they too are simply classified as *Ursus arctos*, like all the conti-nent's other browns and grizzlies. ■

grizzly predation on moose, once said, "For the first couple weeks after calves are born, grizzlies can kill them with impunity." But calves remain highly vulnerable for only a short period: three to four weeks for moose and two to three weeks for caribou. After that, bear predation drops dramatically. Though they can most easily catch and kill sick, injured, or older individuals, grizzlies and brown bears will also take healthy adult hoofed mammals when possible.

In only one sense are browns and grizzlies picky eaters: they prefer the high-energy, high-protein food sources needed to build fat reserves for their long winter dormancy. And they need large quantities of it. Adult bears may consume up to 80 or 90 pounds of food per day during their feeding peak in late summer and autumn, adding 3 to 6 pounds of fat daily.

Because the best foods vary by both season and location, bears must be in the right place at the right time to take advantage of them. Within each of Alaska's major regions, they follow predictable feeding patterns as spring gives way to summer and then fall.

On Kodiak Island, for example, browns initially focus on vegetation. Many graze on sedges and other herbaceous plants found in alpine meadows. Others descend to intertidal beaches to feed on newly emergent plants or the "beach lice" (tiny saltwater organisms) found in kelp beds. Springtime plants are supplemented, when possible, by the bodies of deer that died during the winter or by newborn fawns.

By late June, salmon begin entering Kodiak's streams, and most bears migrate to favorite fishing sites. A few, however, stay in alpine areas, continuing to graze on plants. As berry crops ripen in mid-August, many bears shift to a diet of elderberries and salmonberries. Others mix fish and berries. Fall presents a mixed bag of berries, salmon, roots, and rodents (voles are a favorite) as bears gorge themselves for hibernation.

At the other extreme are the grizzlies of the Arctic. When they first leave their dens, there's little to eat besides overwintered berries or the remains of mammals that died in winter. Green-up

The claws of grizzly and brown bears are ideal for digging.

finally begins in June, and from then through July the bears depend mostly on succulent vegetation such as sedges and Richardson's saxifrage (commonly called "bear flower"), supplemented by the roots of pea-family plants and a variety of rodents: ground squirrels, mice, voles, and lemmings. Caribou calves and, less commonly, adults are occasionally preyed on but are not a critical ingredient in most Arctic bears' diets. Berries, roots, tubers, and rodents are important foods from August into fall, with ground squirrels an especially criti-cal source of calories, along with fish in some places.

SOCIAL LIFE

Brown/grizzly bears were long considered to be solitary creatures, living in isolation from each other except during the mating season. But that simplistic notion has changed.

Females, for example, spend much of their life in family units, with a succession of offspring. Siblings may spend one or more sea-sons in each other's company after weaning. Cubs, adolescents, and even occasional adults demonstrate play behavior. And dozens of individuals sometimes gather in close quarters to feed. Both males and females breed with several partners over the course of a lifetime or even a single season, and such coupled bears may remain together anywhere from a few days to a week or more, when they'll eat, sleep, and travel together.

Based on his many years at the McNeil sanctuary, Larry Aumiller is convinced almost any bear will play: "I've even seen 20-plus-year-old males playing, though that's pretty rare. And I've seen a female with spring cubs [temporarily] abandon its cubs to go off and play with an old buddy." Females also will play with their cubs. Among bears' play activities: wrestling, playing tag, chasing each other in cir-cles, playing with sticks or rocks, sliding down snowbanks.

Social interactions are most obvious within families. But even adult males, which lead a more unsociable lifestyle, share their over-lapping ranges with other bears and participate in group feeds at salmon streams, beached whales, berry patches, or garbage dumps.

When brown bears congregate, a social hierarchy inevitably develops, with dominance based largely on size. Even the biggest males, however, tend to avoid confrontations with females who have cubs. Such females often show great ferocity in protecting their off-spring. Some will fight to the death if necessary. This combativeness may have been an adaptation to life in wide-open spaces during the

Two-year-old brown bear cubs playing.

ice ages, with natural selection favoring females that effectively defended their families in a treeless environment.

Because the personal space of individual bears is inevitably invaded in groups, tension often builds, with stress signaled in a number of ways: yawning, heavy salivation, laid-back ears, body posture, vocalizations (such as growls or huffing), and deliberate movements. Yet only rarely do encounters between stressed-out bears result in fights; less dominant bears are usually given an opportunity to back away. Slowly.

FUTURE OF THE BROWN BEAR

The settlers and developers of the United States nearly wiped out the brown/grizzly bear in the Lower 48, killing the animal whenever possible and destroying its habitat. In Alaska, the great bear has been

Wary of an approaching bear, a female stands up for a better view before quickly moving away.

luckier. Large expanses have been set aside in parks, preserves, refuges, and forests, giving it the space and solitude it needs. Because of the brown bear's demands for space and food, it is sometimes considered an indicator species, one whose well-being serves as a measure of an ecosystem's health.

The state's population of brown/grizzly bears seems secure for now, but the species does face threats. One is human population growth in areas occupied by bears, which inevitably leads to people killing bears that appear to be threatening them or their property. In Southcentral Alaska's Nelchina Basin, homesteaders report "bear problems," because they've moved into grizzly territory. And they want fewer bears. Similar patterns have been observed on the Kenai Peninsula and even the Anchorage area, where human expansion into bear habitat almost inevitably leads to increased conflicts between people and bears and, all too often, dead bears.

The Way Home

Because they live in overlapping ranges, Alaska's brown bears are not considered territorial creatures in the manner of wolves. Yet they do show strong attachments to place when forcibly removed from familiar grounds, and some individuals have demonstrated a remarkable ability to find the way home. One young male in Prince William Sound gave a spectacular demonstration of homing instincts. Transplanted from Cordova, where it had become a nuisance, the bear was taken to Montague Island, more than 40 air miles away. Less than a month later, it had returned to the Cordova dump. To do so, it had to swim a minimum of 5 miles across open water with strong tidal currents. ∎

When Grizzlies and Humans Meet

The great size and strength of the brown/grizzly bear, its fierce nature when protecting its young or its food, and the fact that it's equipped to kill other large mammals have made it a frightening creature to our species. Many people still believe in the simplistic and inaccurate myth of the grizzly as a bloodthirsty animal that lurks in the shadows, waiting to attack anything that crosses its path, humans included.

The truth is that brown/grizzly bears as a rule are wary of humans and avoid them when possible, except when they've learned to associate people with food. They are much more likely to avoid or even flee from humans than to approach them. Even in Anchorage, brown bears regularly roam the community's edges in summer—and sometimes go deep into the city—yet the great majority go unnoticed, because of the animal's wariness of people. The species as a whole is not a predator of humans, and deaths from maulings are uncommon (a total of 50 people in Alaska were killed in bear attacks between 1883 and 2015 according to researcher Tom Smith). Most human injuries and deaths result from sudden, close encounters in which the bear is

A bigger threat comes from resource activities like mining and logging that can endanger bear habitat. The big fear is the cumulative effect of long-term, incremental loss of land the bears depend on. In Southeast Alaska, some bear lands have been compromised by logging and associated road building. On the North Slope, oil and gas projects could eventually fragment their habitat.

Land and wildlife managers need to do long-range planning. Five-year or ten-year plans aren't enough; we need to be thinking at least a century ahead. ■

Brown bear cubs usually stay with their mom until age 2½.

surprised and feels threatened. Once the threat is removed, the assault ends, which is why people are told to "play dead" if attacked during a surprise encounter.

As with other bears, the fact is that we present a much greater threat to them than they do to us. Each year, hundreds are killed in Alaska by trophy hunters, subsistence users, and people who feel threatened, the latter as DLP kills (defense of life and property).

Bear-viewing programs are helping to reshape our knowledge of brown/grizzly bears and our attitudes toward them. At public viewing places in Alaska, the bears have shown they will adapt to, and tolerate, a human presence without harm to either species. The key is that these bears have become habituated to people, but don't associate us with food. Larry Aumiller, retired longtime manager of the McNeil River State Game Sanctuary, once explained "over time it's become clear from their actions that the more tolerant bears perceive us as neutral objects, maybe as innocuous as a rock or a tree." The intolerant ones, meanwhile, leave when humans arrive.

A critical ingredient of safe bear-human interactions is respect for the animal and its great power, and knowledge of its behaviors. By knowing about the bear, we can minimize harmful encounters. ■

TIPS FOR TRAVELING IN BEAR COUNTRY

An aspect of bear behavior that merits special discussion is the animal's alleged unpredictability. Bear specialist Larry Aumiller says the question of whether a bear that encounters a human will charge or flee is predictable "to a certain degree . . . but it requires an understanding of bear behavior. Just like a human, a bear's response depends on many factors: How close are you? What's your behavior? Does the bear have cubs?" But also like humans, bears have differing temperaments—some might be called easygoing; others are more excitable. Different bears are likely to respond with different intensity to perceived threats.

Still, Aumiller stresses, "For the most part, bears are perfectly predictable. For example, a little bear is going to defer to a big bear. And bears will respond to a food source, whether it's salmon or garbage. In the extreme, if you believe that a bear's behavior is totally unpredictable, a result of random choice, then it doesn't really matter what you do in bear country. But that's not the case. There are, in fact, certain precautions, certain actions a person can take to avoid a confrontation, based on what we do know of bears' behavior."

Below are tips for going through bear country:

While hiking or camping:

▶ **Avoid sudden encounters.** Most attacks occur when a bear is surprised or feels threatened. Whenever possible, travel in open country, during daylight hours, and in groups. Make noise when passing through forested areas or thick brush. Talking or singing is preferable to using "bear bells." Leave the family dog at home; dogs can provoke encounters and if a roaming, unleashed dog is chased by a bear, it will likely retreat to its human companion(s), seeking protection—and bringing the bear with it.

Portable electric fences have proven highly effective in protecting property and people from curious bears.

▶ **Keep alert.** Look for signs of bear, such as fresh tracks, scat, matted vegetation, or partly eaten salmon.

▶ **Choose your tent site carefully.** Pitch the tent in open areas, well away from trails, streams with spawning salmon, and berry patches. Avoid places where scavengers have gathered or which have a rotten smell. Bears will often aggressively defend their food supplies.

▶ **Beware of attracting bears with your food.** Cook meals at least 100 feet from tents. Store food away from campsites, hung high between trees whenever possible or placed in bear-resistant containers. And take note that your clothing will carry scents from a day's activities, for instance fishing or hunting. If you've been handling fish or game, change your clothes before entering your tent, and store them away from camp if possible. Avoid odorous foods, and wash up after cooking and eating. Store garbage in an airtight container or where permissible, burn it, and pack out the remains.

▶ **Carry a gun only if you feel comfortable using it in high-stress circumstances.** One alternative is red-pepper spray, which comes in aerosol cans. Because the canisters sometimes leak, it's best to store bear sprays in airtight containers. (Notify pilots that you are carrying bear sprays; a leakage could disable a pilot and lead to a crash. Note that some pilots won't allow canisters inside their aircraft.) Another alternative is flares. Research wildlife ecologist Tom Smith, who's extensively studied bear attacks on humans and done his own field testing of deterrents, says he prefers aerial flares; launched in the bear's direction such a flare presents "a brilliant, red fireball that bears have issues with." The downside, he adds, is that you might start a fire; "but if a bear is breathing down your neck, it's one crisis at a time, bear first, possible fire second."

If you encounter a bear:

▶ Many experts advise that you talk to the bear, to identify yourself as a human. Talk, but don't yell. And don't run. Running from a bear is usually the worst possible action because it will trigger a bear's predatory instincts, and a bear can easily outrun you. Back away slowly, and give the bear an escape route. Avoid getting between a mother and her cubs.

▶ Increase your apparent size. As a rule, bigger is better with bears, which are less likely to attack a larger target. With two or more people, it helps to stand side by side. You might also raise your arms above your head in order to appear larger, and perhaps wave your arms slowly to better identify yourself as human. (In a forested area, it might be appropriate to climb a tree, but remember that black bears and young grizzlies can climb.)

▶ Presenting a minority view but one worth considering given his extensive bear research and fieldwork in Alaska and elsewhere, Tom Smith cautions against talking and waving arms, which he says are "unsubstantiated and dangerous to me." He instead advises people to "stand your ground, group together, and ready your deterrent; give the bear a chance to figure things out; if the bear advances, spray at 20 feet or use other deterrents [such as flare or firearm]."

▶ Play dead if the bear charges and makes contact with you. Fall to the ground, lie flat on your stomach or curl into a ball, hands behind

Bears rely on their keen sense of smell to find food. Campers need to store food and garbage carefully, and cook away from campsites, to avoid problems.

your neck, and remain passive. If you are wearing a pack, leave it on. Once a bear feels there is no longer a threat, the attack will usually end. Wait for the bear to leave before you move. The exception to this rule is when a bear shows predatory behavior. Instead of simply charging, a bear that is actually hunting for prey will show intense interest while approaching at a walk or a run, or by circling, as if stalking you. If you're being treated as prey, fight back. Such circumstances are exceedingly rare and most often involve black bears.

A good summary of bear-safety tips is available in a free brochure titled *Bear Facts*, published jointly by several state and federal agencies in Alaska. Other excellent resources include Stephen Herrero's book *Bear Attacks: Their Causes and Avoidance* and a series of three videos/DVDs developed by the Safety in Bear Country Society (the best known of them is *Staying Safe in Bear Country*). A video has also been produced by the Alaska Department of Fish and Game, aimed at elementary school-age children: *HEY BEARS! How YOU Can Stay Safe in Bear Country.*

IS IT A BROWN BEAR

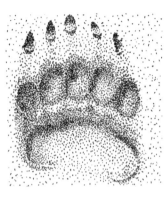

Brown

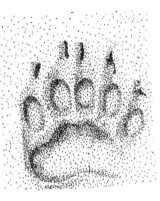

Black

BROWN BEAR

hump

"dishface"

long, fairly
straight claws

OR A BLACK BEAR?

Several physical traits distinguish black bears from brown bears and grizzlies. Color, curiously enough, is not necessarily one of them. Most of Alaska's black bears are indeed black, but some are cinnamon or brown and a few are bluish gray. And some brown bears can look closer to black. Neither is size a dependable distinguishing trait, despite the fact that black bears in general are smaller than brown bears.

It's best to look for the prominent characteristics that mark the difference between the two species. The brown bear has a shoulder hump; the black bear doesn't. Brown bears have a somewhat concave, dish-shaped face; blacks have a straighter profile (a Roman nose).

Black bears have shorter, more curved claws than brown bears, resulting in different tracks. The two species also have different toe imprints. The toes of a black bear show more arc and are more separated than those of a brown, which tend to be close together and more in a line. ■

"Roman nose"

BLACK BEAR

short, curved claws

THE BLACK BEAR

A creature of the forest, the black bear is more secretive and less aggressive than either grizzly or polar bears.

T he smallest and most common of Alaska's three bears, *Ursus americanus* may also be the most enigmatic. A creature largely of forest and shadow, the black bear has followed an evolutionary path that's made it more secretive and less aggressive than the brown bear or polar bear. It moves like a phantom through Alaska's woodlands of spruce and hemlock, cottonwood and birch. Yet for all its wariness—or perhaps because of it—the black bear has proved remarkably adaptable to human development and human intolerance.

The black bear doesn't require vast areas of wilderness to thrive. If there's sufficient food and cover for hiding, members of the species seem equally at home in deep, pristine forests or along the wooded edges of Alaska's largest cities. There the black bear remains mostly invisible—until it develops a taste for human food or garbage. Then the phantom may become a nuisance or even a threat—a problem bear, as we humans put it.

More images to consider. *Ursus americanus* is sometimes called the all-American bear, partly because it lives only in North America (another black bear species, *Ursus thibetanus*, inhabits Asia), but also because it's so common, familiar to people across the continent. Biologists estimate that more than a half million black bears inhabit North America. They range from Canada to Northern Mexico (though not everywhere in between) and are found in about 40 states. Their homelands include arid Southwest chaparral, eastern swamps, Northwest rain forests, and boreal woodlands.

In Alaska, black bears occupy three-quarters of the state, from the Southeast Panhandle to the Brooks Range, though their densities vary greatly, from 10 to 100 animals per 100 square miles, depending on the quality of habitat. The species is absent from unforested mainland regions—the Seward and Alaska Peninsulas, the North Slope, and portions of the Yukon-Kuskokwim Delta—and many islands. When pressed for Alaska's population, some biologists guess 30,000 to 100,000 black bears. Others won't even try. Being a forest animal, the black bear is nearly impossible to census. But on one point, black bear researchers agree: the statewide population is "very healthy."

Here's the irony in all this talk about an all-American bear: for centuries we humans have widely considered the black bear a lesser bruin than its more charismatic relatives. The species' small size and timid nature—at least by ursine standards—account for much of this stereotyping. For some Native peoples, however, the black bear has traditionally been a being of great spiritual power and remains an important subsistence species whose meat is a favored delicacy. Others simply delight in the black bear as a wild creature of the woods.

There is also this paradox: almost always, black bears—even moms with cubs—choose flight over fight when surprised or threatened; but on exceedingly rare occasions, for unknown reasons, a black bear will stalk and kill a person.

As it moves through the forest of our human psyches, the black bear seems to be constantly shifting shapes, changing identities. This confuses us and sometimes frightens us, contributes to flawed notions of the bear's nature, lessens our acceptance of what is really a shy, tolerant animal.

A CREATURE OF THE FOREST

Of North America's three modern bears, only the black is a native species. Both the brown and polar bears evolved into their present-day forms while still in Asia, then later migrated here. But the black bear became what it is today while already inhabiting this continent.

By most accounts, the ancestors of present-day black bears moved from Asia to North America 1 to 4 million years ago, across an early version of the Bering Land Bridge later traveled by humans and brown bears. Those early American settlers were shy, smallish, forest-dwelling omnivores belonging to the species *Ursus etruscus.*

Spread across Asia, Europe, and North America, the Etruscan bears eventually split into three distinct lines. But only one, the black bear line, would survive into the present as a creature of the woods. Like its ancestors, the modern Alaskan black bear is a shy, omnivorous animal, with a body and behavior that reflect adaptations to life in the northern forest—and to the presence of a more dominant competitor, the brown bear.

Consider tree climbing. Adult black bears, unlike their grizzly counterparts, are adept tree climbers. The reason, scientists suspect: during its evolution as a forest creature, the black bear found it easier to retreat from danger than to fight. And the primary escape path it chose was up a tree. To be efficient climbers, black bears maintained a comparatively small body size (though there are notable exceptions

*Black bear cubs are agile climbers and will take
to a tree at the first hint of danger.*

to this rule). And they evolved strong, sharp, narrow, curved claws:
good climbing tools.

Because grizzlies prey on black bears where their ranges overlap, the grizzly's arrival in North America may have reinforced the
black bear's dependence on forest sanctuaries. More than ever, trees
became a refuge critical to its survival.

The black bear's reliance on trees as safe havens is perhaps
best shown by the behavior of females defending their cubs. As
Canadian researcher Stephen Herrero comments in *Bear Attacks*,
"The mother's response when threatened with potential danger will
be to flee with the offspring, to climb a tree with them, or to stay on
the ground and direct aggressive actions toward the intruder while

the cubs find shelter up a tree or in dense vegetation. . . . Trees or dense brush are the core of the mother bear's defense of offspring." Even when defending their cubs, black bear moms seldom attack. Herrero calls them great bluffers and has speculated that they've evolved behaviors to scare off threats without the need of combat.

Females with cubs often seek out the bases of large trees for nursing or sleeping. An Alaskan favorite is the cottonwood, which has deep grooves and is easily climbed. If danger approaches, it's simple for the cubs to scoot up the tree. More rarely, moms will take their young up into a tree for nursing or napping. And sometimes they'll use trees as a kind of babysitter, sending their cubs up high while they go off to feed.

Though tree climbing has evolved as a key survival mechanism, it is also done for recreation and play. Cubs especially like to scramble up and down trees.

And bears of all ages will climb to reach certain foods. Acorns, beechnuts, hickory nuts, hazelnuts, and pine nuts are favorites in the Lower 48, while Alaska's black bears go for aspen and cottonwood buds.

BUILDING FAT RESERVES

Just as forest life has influenced the black bear's physical characteristics and demeanor, these in turn have affected its feeding habits. Besides the fact that they're generally nonaggressive, blacks are also small bears. In Alaska, adult females usually weigh between 120 and 175 pounds, while males range from 200 to 400 pounds. Adult weights vary greatly throughout the black bear's range, depending on quality of habitat, climate, and food supplies. Alaska's biggest black bears are found on Prince of Wales Island; there, large males may weigh 400 to 500 pounds. (The record weight for a North American black bear is 880 pounds, a male killed in North Carolina in 1998; black bear males exceeding 800 pounds have also been documented in Pennsylvania and Canada.)

A Black Bear Can Be Blond

The black bear can be many colors—including brown. Colors range from jet black to chocolate brown, cinnamon, honey, blond, blue, and even white. Even black bears with black coats aren't entirely black: most have brownish muzzles, and many have white to cream-colored V-shaped patches on their chest or throat.

Color variations correlate with habitat and climate. Black is the perfect color for a bear that lives among shadows, like those in moist, densely forested areas. There, the bear itself becomes a shadow in the forest. But earth tones, not shadows, may be more important camouflage in brighter and more open arid regions.

Thus the large majority of black bears east of the Mississippi River are indeed black, as are those in Minnesota and the Pacific Northwest; those in the southwestern United States, however, are mostly brown to blond. In Alaska, as you would expect, the great majority of black bears are in fact black. Less than 10 percent are cinnamon or brown. A tiny fraction have bluish gray coats; these so-called glacier bears are found only along the Gulf of Alaska coast, between Yakutat and Juneau. Even rarer is the white-furred Kermode bear, or spirit bear, which inhabits islands along the British Columbia coast. ■

A cinnamon-colored black bear walks across snow.

Given their retiring nature and smallish though bulky build, it's not surprising that black bears—despite being classified as carnivores—are omnivorous creatures whose diet consists largely of plants, from roots to greens to berries. However, they will prey on animals when possible. Studies conducted on Alaska's Kenai Peninsula indicated that black bears kill up to 35 percent of the region's moose calves each spring. They also eat snowshoe hares, mice, voles, birds and their eggs, insects, and carrion. And in some coastal regions, they'll catch salmon in spawning streams.

Because they'll lose one-fourth to one-half of their body weight while hibernating, Alaska's black bears (like brown bears) must build huge fat reserves in only a few months' time. And in much of their range they must do so on a diet that's largely grasses, sedges, horsetails, insects, and berries. Black bears therefore spend most of their waking hours eating or looking for food. Exceptions, of course, are made during the breeding season.

This doesn't mean black bears consume everything remotely edible; they clearly show a preference for easily digestible and highly nutritional foods. In spring and early summer they seek out young grass shoots and other emerging plants, like horsetails, sedges, wild celery, skunk cabbage, or blue-joint grass. They may also sample catkins, tree buds, overwintered berries, and the roots of some flowers. If carcasses or eggs are available, they'll eat those too, along with ants, wasps, and bees. And as noted above, they'll eat mammals or fish when given the opportunity. Still, some bears don't put on much weight until the really heavy eating begins with the arrival of berry season.

Crowberries, huckleberries, cranberries, and blueberries are Alaskan black bear favorites, but devil's club berries seem to be a special treat. When he worked for the Department of Fish and Game, researcher Chuck Schwartz noted that on the Kenai Peninsula, "I've seen black bears migrate 50 to 70 miles to feed in devil's club patches. It's usually the first abundant producer of fruit and it provides lots of energy. I've tried the berries; they're not palatable to humans, they taste like turpentine. But black bears sure love them." Even when they have access to salmon, black bears will spend considerable time grazing on berries in late summer and fall; studies have shown that a dietary mix of fish and berries works best for bears to gain the weight needed for hibernation.

By late fall, more than half of a bear's body weight will be fat. Once those fat reserves reach a certain level, an internal mechanism shuts off the bear's appetite, and its body chemistry begins adjusting for the long sleep ahead.

INTO THE WINTER DEN

Additional factors, beyond fat reserves, likely influence the time of denning. Food availability is one. Weather conditions and amount of

The Koyukon View

Alaska's Native peoples know the black bear by many names. Different Athabascan groups call it *sis*, *ghedisla*, or *shoh zhraii*, while to the Tlingit it is *s'eek*, to Eyaks, *tsiya*, and to Eskimos, *iyy agriq*. Whatever its given name, the species has traditionally been an important part of Native subsistence culture. The bear's meat is an important food, and its fat, rendered into lard, is used for cooking. In some regions, its hide serves as a mattress or blanket. As anthropologist Richard Nelson reports in his 1983 book *Make Prayers to the Raven*, the black bear also has traditionally ranked high among some tribes as a ceremonial delicacy and a spirit being. Among the Koyukon Athabascan of Alaska's northern Interior, says Nelson, it "takes us near the apex of power among spirits of the natural world," below only the grizzly and wolverine.

Nelson's story about the Koyukon people documents the traditional relationship of one Native tribe with the black bear, whom the Koyukon know as *sis*. "Their knowledge of these animals is deep and detailed," he explains, "their hunting methods sophisticated and complex. . . ." And their respect for the bear's spirit is immense. For that reason the hunt has by long custom been a quest for prestige as well as food, an expression of manhood. Because its spirit is so potent, "People's behavior toward black bears is subject to an extraordinary number of taboos."

It's important to recognize that many taboos, customs, and beliefs are not as strictly followed nowadays, and both attitudes and practices have changed considerably in some Native villages (at least partly because of more advanced technology). Still, it's worth noting what Nelson learned from his Koyukon teachers as recently as the mid-1970s.

"Disregarding or violating bear taboos can be sharply punished," he notes in his book. "Ordinary offenses alienate the animal, make it elusive or invisible. . . . More serious offenses can bring illness to the person or a family member, or even death. Insulting comments or gestures toward the animal, whether it is dead or alive, rank among the most severe transgressions. Bear attacks, which are exceedingly rare, may be interpreted as retaliation for such insults."

Koyukon women traditionally faced the most taboos. They were

not to speak the black bear's name, instead calling it *hulzinh* ("dark one") to keep from offending its spirit. They weren't allowed to hunt bears and had to avoid even looking at a black bear.

Hunters, too, had to be careful not to offend the bear. When speaking about a denning bear he found, a man would discuss his discovery using indirect words. Cryptic language is even more important when a bear is killed, because speaking directly about the kill would offend its spirit. A successful hunter might simply remark, "I found something in a hole."

Elaborate rules customarily governed the treatment of a dead bear's remains. If killed in a den, it must be pulled out "the old way," by hand or rope, and then immediately skinned and butchered. The head is removed and hung in a nearby tree or burned, and the hide handled carefully, because bear skins keep their life force for several years. The use of various internal organs is also governed by rules; for instance, no one should eat the first neck joint, because it causes slowness, as reflected in the way a bear moves its head slowly.

A few days after a bear was killed, men and boys would gather for a ceremonial feast, a "bear party." Held in the woods, away from female influence, the feast is "a memorial potlatch held to honor the killed animal."

The final mark of respect is proper disposal of its bones; usually that means burning them in a clean fire. ■

daylight are others. The timing varies from region to region and year to year, but most bears enter their dens by late October or early November and, with few exceptions, they remain there until April or May. As with brown bears, pregnant females den earliest and emerge latest, while adult males have the shortest denning period. On average, Alaska's black bears annually spend 190 to 230 days denned up.

Black bears make their dens in almost every imaginable place. They've been found in hollow trees, caves, brush piles, highway culverts, and even under houses. Not far outside Anchorage, biologists once found five bears—two adults and three cubs—squeezed into what Department of Fish and Game researcher Sean Farley described as a "rock den," no more than 30 yards from the Seward Highway.

On the Kenai Peninsula, more than 90 percent are ground excavations on gentle slopes, within upland forest. In other regions of Alaska, however, half or less of the dens that biologists have discovered were excavations.

When he worked for the state of Alaska, bear biologist Sterling Miller discovered one den in a Susitna Valley cliff. The opening was a narrow crack and "you had to crawl in 20 feet before you reached a nice, big nesting chamber." Another bear climbed 30 feet inside a hollow cottonwood, while one crawled among a jumble of boulders. Some of the dens have probably been used for centuries (though it's rare for an individual bear to return to the same site in consecutive years) and have thick, comfortable—at least to a bear—mats of grass. At the other extreme are excavated dens that last only a single season.

In the Tanana Flats region near Fairbanks, bear researcher John Hechtel once found three surface nests in a single season. "Each of the bears had dug a shallow trench, just a few inches deep, and let the snow drift over them," he recalls. "One of them wasn't much more than an ice bubble when I saw it." Those are among the stranger denning choices, given the region's severe and prolonged winters. Another female piled dried grass into a haystack-like

In Southeast Alaska a black bear wades into a stream to fish for pink salmon.

mound, then burrowed into it with her three 2-year-old cubs. As in other areas, most of the Tanana Flats bears built insulating nests in their dens, using grass, leaves, and twigs, but a few slept on bare dirt. And some denning bears observed in early spring were lying on wet, muddy ground.

THE LONG SLEEP

As a species, the American black bear was born sometime during the Pleistocene ice age, so its evolution has been shaped by seasonal cold and associated food shortages, as well as forest life. One adaptation is the bear's thick coat. Others are its bulky body and ability

When Black Bears and Humans Meet

Black bears don't share the reputation of the brown/grizzly bear for ferocity. Over the years, they've injured many more people than brown bears have, but more than 90 percent of those injuries were minor, while injuries from brown bears are usually serious. More notable than the black bear's occasional aggression is its restraint. Given the large population of North American black bears, attacks happen very seldom. Most occur when people feed the bears, tease them, poke them, or even try to pet them or shake hands with them.

Unlike encounters with grizzlies, surprise meetings with black bears—even moms with cubs—rarely lead to injury. Some experts suggest backing away quietly during close encounters, while others recommend mild human aggression: assuming a dominant posture and speaking assertively, in a calm voice, while giving the bear room to escape. In the unlikely case of a mom attacking to defend her cubs, passive resistance—playing dead—is best.

On rare occasions, some black bears appear to treat humans as prey. Stephen Herrero, author of *Bear Attacks*, says predatory behavior most commonly associated with wild black bears in rural or remote areas where they have relatively little association with people. In other words, in areas similar to much of Alaska. "A typical predation scenario," Herrero writes, "might involve the bear slowly approaching a person during the day, perhaps partly circling and then rushing toward the person, trying to knock the intended prey down and inflicting injuries. . . . "

A black bear hunting its prey will continue the attack until the prey escapes or dies. Thus if you suspect a black bear considers you its prey, do not play dead. Instead, fight back, hitting the bear in the face—the nose a prime target—with whatever weapon you have: firearms, an ax, a large piece of wood, a rock, your fists. But to put these rare cases of black bear aggression into context, consider this: despite the many thousands of encounters between the species each year, researcher Tom Smith found that only six people have been killed by black bears in Alaska since 1883. In short, you're far more likely to be killed by another human than by a black bear—or any bear, for that matter. ∎

to store large amounts of fat. But its most marvelous mechanism is hibernation.

Many northern mammals—ground squirrels, marmots, woodchucks, chipmunks, bats—enter a deep sleep to survive winter's dearth of food. But bears have evolved physiological mechanisms unlike any other creature.

Alaska's black bears and brown bears may den for more than half of each year, without the need to defecate, urinate, eat, or drink for long stretches of time. Yet unlike rodent hibernators, which enter a death-like torpor, their body temperature and metabolic rates drop only slightly and bears will sometimes waken from their sleep; females with newborn cubs are especially light sleepers, given the need to feed their young several times daily. Bears may even occasionally leave their dens and go on walks, then return. By winter's end they may lose 25 to 50 percent of their body weight; but for healthy bears, the loss is all, or nearly all, fat. And they show no recognizable signs of muscle atrophy or bone degeneration.

Even more extraordinary is the fact that pregnant bears give birth during this extended period of fasting and then nurse their cubs for several months while still in hibernation. The cycle of ursine pregnancy begins with early to midsummer mating (at age 4 or older for Alaska's black bears). Through a mechanism called delayed implantation, fertilized eggs remain detached from the female's uterus until early winter, thus delaying embryo development by several months. If a female hasn't added enough fat to get herself and a litter of cubs through the winter, the pregnancy is terminated.

After a two-month gestation period, between one and six black bear cubs are born in January or February. In Alaska, litters with more than three cubs are rare; the usual size is two. About the size of a chipmunk, newborn black bear cubs are toothless, sightless, and nearly hairless, and weigh ½ pound. According to Farley, the state biologist, they're born at such an early stage for a good reason: there are biochemical restraints that prevent a fasting bear from pro-

A black bear stands in an alder patch and marks branches.

viding healthy nutrition in utero; those difficulties can be bypassed by ex-utero nursing, even when the young are helpless and hairless. The den acts as a kind of surrogate womb, providing warmth and protection.

Upon giving birth, the mother licks her newborns and eats the afterbirth to keep the den clean and eliminate odors that might attract predators. The precautions are well taken: grizzlies, humans, and even wolves are known to kill and eat hibernating black bears. For similar reasons, the mom will also eat the cubs' feces and lick up their urine. By consuming her cubs' waste, she also recovers some of the fluids lost by nursing.

Among the more intriguing studies of Alaska's hibernating black bears were those done in the early 1990s by Brian Barnes and others in the University of Alaska's Institute of Arctic Biology. Among the findings: despite outside temperatures that fell to −58°F, the sleeping bears' core temperature never dropped below 86°. Moreover, core body temperatures showed multiday rhythms in which they would cool to 86°, then rewarm, and gradually cool again. Exactly how the bears kept their body temperature from falling below 86°, and how they rewarmed themselves, remains a mystery.

The observed hibernating bears spent 90 percent of their time asleep. From January through March, they awakened only during a week of severe cold and when researchers made noises outside the den to test the bears' alertness. Other hibernators, such as ground squirrels, periodically rouse themselves and bring heart rates and body temperatures back to normal. Bears as a rule apparently don't need to do so, though as noted above, females with newborns will stir for nursing.

THE YOUNG BEARS

When a black bear mother and her family finally leave their den in spring, the cubs will have gained 4 to 8 pounds. And by summer's end, they'll weigh in the neighborhood of 30 pounds—if they survive. Anywhere from 30 to 45 percent of Alaska's black bear cubs die before their first birthday. Some starve. Others drown, fall from trees, or get eaten by wolves, lynx, or other bears. While cannibalism by other black bears occurs, it doesn't appear common; grizzlies are a much greater threat.

Black bear cubs are normally weaned when they're 1½ years old, sooner than either grizzlies or polar bears. But in Northern

Alaska, many females apparently keep their cubs an extra year, perhaps to help them survive in a more severe climate.

Learning to live without Mom is an imposing task, and mortality rates for newly weaned black bear adolescents approach those for first-year cubs. Those skilled or lucky enough to reach adulthood face few dangers besides grizzlies and humans, and some survive into their 20s. Most, however, don't make it past their mid-teens.

Though they may become wanderers when first separated from their mothers, black bears, like others of their kind, eventually settle into home ranges, where they'll spend the rest of their days. Females generally stay close, in areas that overlap with their mother's home range, while males disperse widely. Because they travel into unfamiliar territory inhabited by other bears or humans, many male adolescents die before establishing a home range.

Range sizes vary greatly throughout Alaska: some are as small as 1 to 2 square miles, others exceed 200 square miles. Male black bears, like their grizzly counterparts, inhabit a much larger area than females, for both breeding and feeding purposes. The smallest are those occupied by females with newborn cubs.

Like polar bears and brown bears, black bears will display some social behaviors in the form of play, limited family ties (mainly between mother and cubs, until weaning), and occasional group feeds.

FUTURE OF THE BLACK BEAR

Alaska's black bear population is in very good shape because of the species' large numbers, its adaptability to humans, and abundant habitat. Hunting is regulated to maintain a healthy population. Poaching for black bear parts, such as gall bladders and bear paws, has not been a problem in Alaska as it has in Asia, parts of Canada, and the Lower 48, though at times there has been some evidence of black bear poaching in Alaska. Strong penalties are necessary to minimize such illegal killing.

A black bear forages on barnacles and other intertidal foods.

Alaska remains blessed with expansive forested areas that provide the cover and food black bears need to thrive, so the species is under no immediate threat. But biologists warn against complacency in the future, especially in developed areas, where conflicts between land use by humans and the needs of bears will be the greatest. ■

VIEWING ALASKA'S BEARS

Among the many people—both residents and visitors—who annually participate in adventure travel and wildlife watching, thousands visit Alaska's backcountry each summer hoping to see bears. They can be viewed throughout most of the state from May through September, but some areas naturally offer better opportunities than others.

One of the most popular places to view grizzlies is Denali National Park, where they are frequently seen by summer visitors, whether exploring the wilderness on foot and/or traveling the park's lone road on shuttle and tour buses. Commercial operators nowadays conduct brown bear–viewing tours in many coastal areas, from the Southeast Panhandle to the most remote reaches of the Alaska Peninsula in Southwest Alaska. Whether on tours or traveling independently, backcountry explorers are likely to see brown/grizzly bears—preferably from a distance—in many of Alaska's protected wildlands, for instance Glacier Bay, Katmai, and Wrangell–St. Elias National Parks, the Tongass and Chugach National Forests, and the

Kenai, Kodiak, Becharof, and Arctic National Wildlife Refuges, as well as the Chugach, Wood-Tikchik, and other state parks.

Black bears tend to be more secretive than brown bears and they prefer forests to open tundra or coastline; plus they rarely gather in large numbers as brown bears do in some salmon-rich coastal areas. They are therefore less visible than their larger and more aggressive relatives; still, black bears may be encountered in wooded wildlands and along trails and roads in many Alaska regions, including more urban areas.

Polar bears are seen even less frequently, as they prefer the seldom-visited pack ice and nearby Arctic shores. The best place to see them in Alaska is near the remote Iñupiat village of Kaktovik, where polar bears congregate in fall and early winter to feed on whale carcasses left over from subsistence hunts. Though it involves long-distance travel by plane, and both travel and lodging is expensive, since the early 2000s this rare gathering has drawn a growing number of bear watchers.

PRIME VIEWING SITES

Except for females who have cubs, adult bears tend to lead largely solitary lives. Males, in particular, seldom engage in social behavior, except during mating season. For them to gather in large numbers and in close quarters is therefore exceptional. That they might do so while viewed by humans is even more amazing, given their natural wariness. Yet each summer, in scattered areas throughout Alaska's southern coastal regions, bears do come together in large groups. What draws them together and demands their tolerance of each other—and in some instances, of a human audience—is an abundant, concentrated, and energy-rich food source: salmon.

Of the hundreds of Alaska salmon streams where bears congregate, a few have become places where people gather as well. They come to watch, take photographs, and spend time in the company of creatures symbolic of Alaska's wildness. A couple of bear-viewing

*A guided photography group in Katmai National Park
watches a passing bear and her cubs.*

sites were established in Southeast Alaska in the early 1900s, but
they attracted few people. Not until McNeil River State Game
Sanctuary gained widespread acclaim in the 1970s and 1980s as a
place for nonscientists to observe "bears being bears" did the public
begin actively seeking out these special sites.

Four of Alaska's wild places have become especially well
known for their bear-viewing programs. At most of these sites, people come to see brown bears. A notable exception is Anan Creek,
known for its rare congregation of black bears.

Because bears at these sites have become habituated to
humans, they sometimes wander close enough that you can smell
their dank fur, hear the loud crunching as they tear at salmon flesh
and bone, see the scars that streak their faces and bodies, hear their

panting breaths. It's closer than you'd ever want to get while exploring the wilderness on your own; but here, watching from a viewing platform or accompanied by knowledgeable guides, it's safe to watch, listen, enjoy—as long as you obey the rules. These are still wild animals.

The nature of these places and the way they're managed vary greatly. But as McNeil's former longtime manager, Larry Aumiller, once said, all of them teach a critically important lesson: when things are done right, bears and humans can indeed peacefully coexist.

MCNEIL RIVER

The McNeil River State Game Sanctuary is the standard by which all other bear-viewing areas are measured. Established in 1967 and managed by the state's Division of Wildlife Conservation, this sanctuary on the Alaska Peninsula protects what is widely considered the world's largest gathering of brown bears.

Brown bear with a red salmon caught in Mikfik Creek, near McNeil River.

The focal point of the gathering is McNeil Falls, where bears come to feed on chum salmon. During the peak of that July–August chum run, dozens of brown bears congregate. As many as 144 individual bears (adults and cubs) have been identified along the river in a single season. And biologists have counted more than 70 bears at the falls at one time (though 30 to 60 is more common during the prime viewing period).

Even more impressive than the numbers of bears, perhaps, is their acceptance of a human presence. "Think about it," says Larry Aumiller, who managed McNeil for three decades, starting in the mid-1970s. "You've got this group of 11 or 12 people standing in the middle of 40, 50, 60 bears. You're very close to where they want to be. And they tolerate you." Some will eat salmon, take naps, nurse cubs, or even mate within a short distance of the visitor viewing pads.

A key ingredient of McNeil's success is people management. Only 10 people per day, accompanied by one or two sanctuary guides, are allowed to visit McNeil Falls and other areas where "the bears come first." Once there, bear watchers are restricted to a defined viewing area. And they keep to a set schedule. In this way, people become predictable to the bears. The other crucial element: McNeil's bears view humans as neutral objects. People don't pose a threat, nor are they a source of food.

Until the mid-1980s, few people visited the sanctuary before July 1. But a new pattern emerged when a June sockeye run began to increase dramatically at Mikfik Creek, a small neighboring stream of McNeil. Not surprisingly, more and more bears were lured by Mikfik's improved fishing opportunities—and following the bears were wildlife photographers. Mikfik's popularity prompted the state to expand its permit period, which now runs from early June through late August.

While Mikfik has made the sanctuary's bear-viewing more diverse, McNeil Falls remains the primary focus in July and much of August. A mile above McNeil's mouth, it's a steplike series of small waterfalls, pools, and rapids. Individual bears take up fishing positions based on their place in the ursine pecking order. Prime spots are located along the western bank, opposite the two viewing pads. Here the most dominant bears—adult males, some weighing 1,000 pounds or more—jockey for position.

The bears use a variety of fishing techniques. Some stand motionless, patiently monitoring the river. When a chum swims by, the bear pins it to the stream bottom with its paws, then bites it. Others use snorkeling techniques, and a few even dive for fish. The chum run ends by mid- to late August, but the bears begin to disperse even before then, as they go in search of another nutritious food: berries.

Getting there: The McNeil River State Game Sanctuary is on the upper Alaska Peninsula, 250 miles southwest of Anchorage. Most visitors fly in, using floatplane services based in Homer.

Manager: Alaska Department of Fish and Game.

Prime viewing: June through mid-August.

Visitor limits: Ten people, accompanied by sanctuary staff, per day. Permit applications must be received by March 1; winners are determined by lottery.

Overnight facilities: Spaces provided for tent camping.

Information: Alaska Department of Fish and Game, Division of Wildlife Conservation, 333 Raspberry Road, Anchorage, AK 99518-1599; (907) 267-2189; e-mail dfg.dwc.mcneil-info@alaska.gov; *Website:* www.adfg.alaska.gov/index.cfm?adfg=mcneilriver.main.

··

PACK CREEK

Admiralty Island, within Tongass National Forest in Southeast Alaska, has long been recognized as an important brown bear refuge. The Tlingit people who first lived here called it *kootznoowoo*, "fortress of the bears"—a fitting description for one of North America's richest bear habitats.

Ninety-six miles long, with 678 miles of coastline, dozens of salmon streams, and forested mountains, Admiralty Island is home to 1,500 or more bears, or about one for each of its 1,644 square miles. Few places in the world have higher densities.

On the east side of Admiralty is Pack Creek, the region's premier bear-watching site. Pack Creek's special niche can be traced to the early 1930s, when the drainage was closed to bear hunting (a closure that has since been expanded to about 95 square miles). One year later, the Civilian Conservation Corps built a platform above the creek to aid bear viewing.

Still, Pack Creek had few bears until Stan Price settled there in the mid-1950s. Nicknamed Stan the Bear Man, Price became a local legend because of his unusual friendship with bears. He took in several orphaned cubs and raised them as pets. And contrary to state regulations, he fed bears on his homestead. Inevitably the number of bears grew. Price died in 1989, but the bears have remained. Between two and three dozen brown bears now regularly use Pack Creek, though only the most tolerant ones—an estimated 15 to 20 individuals—are seen by visitors.

Part of both the 60,800-acre Stan Price State Wildlife Sanctuary and Admiralty Island National Monument's Kootznoowoo Wilderness, Pack Creek is managed cooperatively by the Alaska Department of Fish and Game and US Forest Service, as a day-use area. Visitors are greeted by a ranger and given an orientation and safety talk. Following that talk, permit holders are turned loose, though viewing options are limited: bear-watching is allowed only at a sand spit near the creek mouth and an upstream observation tower, both reached by well-defined paths. Visitors are reminded that Pack Creek is part of a designated wilderness area, so they should not expect visitor amenities; they must also store and eat their food at a designated picnic area and stay on defined travel routes. The presence of 5 to 8 bears at one time is considered a good viewing day.

Getting there: Pack Creek is on Admiralty Island, within Tongass National Forest, 40 miles south of Juneau. It can be reached by either boat or air (it's about a half hour from Juneau by floatplane).

Managers: Alaska Department of Fish and Game and US Forest Service.

Prime viewing: Late July through mid-August.

Visitor limits and permits: Twenty-four people per day during the peak period of July 5 to August 25; permits and reservations issued on a first-come, first-served basis beginning February 1 each year. Permits are also required during the nonpeak shoulder periods from June 1 to July 4 and from August 26 to September 10, but reservations aren't required and there is no visitor cap, though groups are restricted to 12 people. The shoulder season dates are expected to eventually shift to include late May and eliminate September. Permits must be obtained through the recreation.gov website or by calling 877-444-6777.

Overnight facilities: None.

Information: Admiralty Island National Monument, 8510 Mendenhall Loop Road, Juneau, AK 99801; (907) 586-8800. *Website:* www.fs.usda.gov/detail/tongass/recreation/natureviewing/?cid=stelprdb5401876.

....

ANAN CREEK

Each summer, as they do in forest streams throughout Southeast Alaska, dozens of bears fish Anan Creek for salmon. What's different here is that both brown and black bears use the creek; normally, blacks tend to avoid the larger and more aggressive browns.

Even more unusual, from a bear-viewing perspective, is the fact that the black bears are the chief attraction at the Anan Wildlife Observatory. They're easily observed during the daylight hours, while Anan's brown bears are normally best seen early in the morning or late at night.

Anan Creek, in Tongass National Forest, has been locally

known for its gathering of black bears since the early 1900s. Each summer, dozens of black bears are drawn here by one of the region's largest pink salmon runs. Working among moss-covered granite boulders that border the tea-colored stream, bears grab their prey from pools along the shore.

Upon catching a fish, most of Anan's black bears retreat into the creekside boulder piles or scurry into the thick forest understory. It's uncommon to see more than a handful at any one time, but bear researchers say that Anan is nevertheless one of the best spots in North America to watch *Ursus americanus.*

A viewing platform was first built at Anan in the 1930s, but the creek required only minimal management until the 1990s, when annual visitation jumped from fewer than 1,000 to nearly 4,000 people. In response, the Forest Service built a modern "observatory" that includes a partly sheltered observation deck, viewing blind, and quarter-mile boardwalk that connects the viewing site to the beach.

The agency also put a number of restrictions into place. Chief among them: permits are required during the July 5 to August 25 peak season and food is prohibited beyond the trailhead. As at Pack Creek, visitors are greeted and given a safety orientation and then allowed to walk unescorted, but must stay on designated trails and the observatory platform. The principal viewing site overlooks the creek and falls, which tumble through a narrow, forest-enclosed gorge.

Getting there: The Anan Wildlife Observatory is in Southeast Alaska's Tongass National Forest, about 30 miles southeast of Wrangell. It's accessible by either boat or floatplane.

Manager: US Forest Service.

Prime viewing: July through late August.

Visitor limits and permits: Visitation is restricted to 60 people per day during the designated July 5 to August 25 peak season. Permits must be obtained in advance, through the recreation.gov website or by calling 877-444-6777.

Overnight facilities: A public-use cabin is located about a mile from the observatory; it's very popular in summer and must be reserved in advance. No camping is permitted in the area.

Information: US Forest Service, Wrangell Ranger District, PO Box 51, Wrangell, AK 99929; (907) 874-2323. *Website:* www.fs.usda.gov/detail/r10/specialplaces/?cid=fsbdev2_038752

....

BROOKS FALLS

The ritual begins in early July, with the return of the sockeyes. Thousands of bright silvery fish enter the Brooks River and push their way upstream toward spawning grounds in Brooks Lake. Nearing the end of their journey from the sea, they face one final obstacle: a 6-foot-high falls. Hundreds of sockeyes school in the pools below as they wait their turn to jump.

Following the salmon to Brooks Falls are brown bears. As many as two dozen may compete for fishing spots here in July, grabbing sockeye from atop the falls, snorkeling in the pools below, or watching from stream banks, waiting for scraps. Also watching are 40 people, squeezed together on an elevated platform built along the river's south shore.

A 1½-mile-long clear-water stream that connects Brooks and Naknek Lakes, the Brooks River is located within 4-million-acre Katmai National Park and Preserve. Since the 1980s, this small Alaska Peninsula stream has been recognized as one of the state's premier bear-viewing sites. During the July peak, bears often fish within 50 feet of the falls viewing platform. They can also be watched from a second platform below the falls in the "ripples" area and at one located near the mouth of the river (a good place to see moms with their cubs). They may even be encountered in Brooks Camp, a nearby developed area that includes a lodge, cabins, visitor center, and campground.

Brooks Camp got its start in 1950 as a sportfishing destination. Then it was rare to see bears along the Brooks River because they were chased away or shot, first by Native inhabitants of the region and later by anglers. A dramatic, albeit gradual change occurred when the National Park Service began to actively manage the area in the 1950s. Within three decades Brooks Camp was transformed from a little-known fisherman's paradise into a world-renowned bear-watcher's haven. Nowadays, at the peak of the July salmon run, 40 or more brown bears (not including cubs) inhabit the Brooks River drainage. A second, smaller gathering occurs in September, when bears come to feed on the dead, "spawned-out" salmon that collect in the lower river.

Visitors must attend a "bear etiquette" talk when they arrive and obey a series of rules, but for the most part they're on their own. Up to 300 people may pass through the Brooks Falls platforms daily, including day-trippers who fly in for a few hours of bear watching. By summer's end, 10,000 people from around the world will have visited (the majority in July).

Brown bear atop Brooks Falls with a fresh-caught red salmon.

To make things easier on both people and bears along the heavily traveled lower river, an elevated bridge and more than 2,000 feet of new boardwalk are scheduled to be completed by the summer of 2017.

Getting there: Brooks Falls and nearby Brooks Camp are in Katmai National Park and Preserve, 300 miles southwest of Anchorage. Most visitors fly, via commercial airline, to King Salmon, then take a floatplane to Brooks.

Manager: National Park Service.

Prime viewing: July and September.

Visitor limits: None for day visits; overnight visitors are limited by what the lodge and campground can hold.

Overnight facilities: Brooks Lodge, owned by Katmailand, Inc., of Anchorage, phone (800) 544-0551, e-mail info@katmailand.com; *Website:* www.katmailand.com/travel-tours/bearviewing. There's also a Park Service campground; sites must be reserved in advance either through the recreation.gov website or by calling 877-444-6777. Those who wish to apply for a campground site should note that they are completely filled within minutes, for the peak period of July.

Information: Katmai National Park, P.O. Box 7, King Salmon, AK 99613; (907) 246-3305. *Website:* www.nps.gov/katm/planyour-visit/bear-watching.htm

Brooks River Bearcams: Those unable to visit the Brooks River can still watch its bears in action via webcams stationed along the river and in nearby areas: www.nps.gov/katm/learn/photosmulti-media/webcams.htm

SUGGESTED READING

Bledsoe, Thomas. *Brown Bear Summer: Life Among Alaska's Giants*. New York: Truman Talley Books, 1987.

Craighead, Frank C. *Track of the Grizzly*. San Francisco: Sierra Club Books, 1979.

Davids, Richard C., and Dan Guravich. *Lords of the Arctic: A Journey Among the Polar Bears*. New York: Macmillan, 1982.

DeRocher, Andrew. *Polar Bears: A Complete Guide to their Biology and Behavior*. Baltimore: Johns Hopkins University Press, 2012.

Dewey, Donald. *Bears*. New York: Gallery Books, 1991.

Dufresne, Frank. *No Room for Bears*. Portland, OR: Alaska Northwest Books, 1991.

Fair, Jeff. *The Great American Bear*. Minocqua, WI: Northward Press, 1990.

Furtman, Michael. *Black Bear Country*. Minocqua, WI: Northward Press, 1998.

Herrero, Stephen. *Bear Attacks: Their Causes and Avoidance*. New York: Nick Lyons Books, first edition, 1985; revised and updated edition, 2002.

Jans, Nick. *The Grizzly Maze: Timothy Treadwell's Fatal Obsession with Alaskan Bears*. New York: Dutton, 2005.

Illingworth, Frank. *Wild Life Beyond the North*. New York: Charles Scribner's Sons, 1952.

Lopez, Barry. *Arctic Dreams: Imagination and Desire in a Northern Landscape*. New York: Charles Scribner's Sons, 1986.

Lynch, Wayne. *Bears: Monarchs of the Northern Wilderness*. Seattle: The Mountaineers, 1993.

Masterson, Linda. *Living with Bears: A Practical Guide to Bear Country*. Masonville, CO: PixyJack Press, 2006.

McNamee, Thomas. *The Grizzly Bear*. New York: Alfred A. Knopf, 1984.

Mulvaney, Kieran. *The Great White Bear: A Natural and Unnatural History of the Polar Bear*. New York: Houghton Mifflin Harcourt, 2011.

Murie, Adolph. *The Grizzlies of Mount McKinley*. Seattle: University of Washington Press, 1985.

Murray, John A., ed. *The Great Bear: Contemporary Writings on the Grizzly*. Portland, OR: Alaska Northwest Books, 1992.

Nelson, Richard. *Hunters of the Northern Ice*. Chicago: University of Chicago Press, 1969.

———· *Make Prayers to the Raven: A Koyukon View of the Northern Forest.* Chicago: University of Chicago Press, 1983.

Payton, Brian. *Shadow of the Bear: Travels in Vanishing Wilderness.* New York: Bloomsbury Publishing, 2006.

Perry, Richard. *The World of the Polar Bear.* Seattle: University of Washington Press, 1966.

Rennick, Penny, ed. *Alaska's Bears.* Anchorage: Alaska Geographic Society, 1993.

Rennicke, Jeff. *Bears of Alaska in Life and Legend.* Boulder, CO: Roberts Rinehart Publishers, 1987.

Rockwell, David. *Giving Voice to Bear: Northern American Indian Myths, Rituals, and Images of Bear.* Niwot, CO: Roberts Rinehart Publishers, 1991.

Russell, Andy. *Grizzly Country.* New York: Alfred A. Knopf, 1967.

Savage, Candace. *Grizzly Bears.* San Francisco: Sierra Club Books, 1990.

Seton, Ernest Thompson. *The Biography of a Grizzly.* New York: Grosset and Dunlap, 1899.

Shepard, Paul, and Barry Sanders. *The Sacred Paw: The Bear in Nature, Myth, and Literature.* New York: Penguin Books, 1985.

Simpson, Sherry. *Dominion of Bears: Living with Wildlife in Alaska.* Lawrence: The University Press of Kansas, 2013.

Smith, Dave. *Backcountry Bear Basics: The Definitive Guide to Avoiding Unpleasant Encounters.* Seattle: The Mountaineers, 1997.

Stirling, Ian, ed. *Bears: Majestic Creatures of the Wild.* Emmaus, PA: Rodale Press, 1993.

———· *Polar Bears: The Natural History of a Threatened Species.* Markham, Ontario: Fitzhenry & Whiteside, 2011.

Stirling, Ian, and Dan Guravich. *Polar Bears.* Ann Arbor: University of Michigan Press, 1990.

Taylor, Dave. *Black Bears: A Natural History.* Markham, Ontario: Fitzhenry & Whiteside, 2006.

Troyer, Will. *Into Brown Bear Country.* Fairbanks: University of Alaska Press, 2005.

———· *Bear Wrangler: Memoirs of an Alaska Pioneer Biologist.* Fairbanks: University of Alaska Press, 2008.

Walker, Tom, and Larry Aumiller. *The Way of the Grizzly: The Bears of Alaska's Famed McNeil River.* Stillwater, MN: Voyageur Press, 1998. First published as *River of Bears* in 1993 by Voyageur Press.

Online/Internet reference: International Association for Bear Research and Management, www.bearbiology.com

INDEX

Page locators in *italics* indicate maps and photographs.

Printed in the USA
CPSIA information can be obtained
at www.ICGtesting.com
JSHW072028140824
68134JS00044B/3836

9 781943 328581